Considering Jesus

by

Dan Gallagher

ISBN# 978-0-9628971-7-7
First Edition © 2016

Spirit & Truth Fellowship International®
180 Robert Curry Drive
Martinsville, IN 46151
888.255.6189, M-F 9 to 5
STF@STFonline.org
STFonline.org

Printed in the United States of America.

"If the whole universe has no meaning, we should never have found out it has no meaning."

- C. S. Lewis

Table of Contents

Acknowledgments

One of the benefits of age is that the older we grow, the more of life we experience, which for many people means we learn from our failures and successes and develop a deeper sense of the importance of life. This book is my attempt to help others sort through the clutter and noise of the world around us so that they may be able to see what is necessary to have a truly meaningful life.

A special word of thanks to my wife, Lori, for her encouragement and the countless conversations that helped me to sort and organize in my mind the many concepts in this book. I also owe a deep gratitude to my friend and coworker John Schoenheit, a man who I consider in many ways to be my mentor and upon whose shoulders I so often stand. I also must give special thanks to my main editor, Renee Dugan, for her dedication and constant encouragement. Great gratitude is also expressed for Jerry Wierwille and the tremendous insights and clarifications he provided, Janet Speakes for her masterful editing, Ryan Maher for his encouragement, coaching, and cover art participation, Dustin Williams for a wonderful job at layout and production, and lastly for Andy Trimble and John Sandt for their insights and encouragement.

Dedication

This work is dedicated to my daughters, Maureen, Cassie, and Cathryn, and most especially to my precious Sheila, whose life and death taught me the importance of living a life with purpose and genuine meaning.

Introduction

What's most important to you? What's the most valuable thing you have? We all have our stuff, the things that we are attached to. Generally, they are things that make us feel valuable, or possibly connected to others. I have a ring that my dad gave me before he died, somewhat of a family heirloom. I love the ring because it makes me feel connected to him and my heritage. But in spite of how sentimental I am about the ring, no material possession is most important to me.

The odds are that, like me, "stuff" is not the most important thing in your life either. I imagine that there are some people who would say their careers, reputations, or even their savings are pretty important to them. But even these don't compare to the value we place upon people.

If you're married, then you probably consider your spouse, or your children, as what is most important in your life; and if you aren't, then possibly it is your parents, siblings, or closest friends. In any case, most people consider other people as most important in their life.

I believe the best answer to the question is that "YOU" are the most valuable thing in *your life*. After all, if there were no *you* then there would be no relationships with others (or stuff) for *you* to enjoy. In other words, your life is the most precious thing you have, and most especially since you only get one.

We all come into this world much like a blank slate, and we begin to write upon it the things we experience and are taught. All the good, the bad, and the ugly are etched upon the chalkboard of our lives. The way we think and behave, our internal belief systems and outlook on life are conditioned by the drawings on the chalkboard. Since part of what is drawn there is what we believe, it is imperative that we stop and consider why we believe it. This is the one and only life we have; therefore we owe it to ourselves to challenge our biases and to consider the deep questions about who we are, why we are here, and what our lives mean. These are the questions we must ask ourselves about the meaning and purpose of our existence.

In considering these questions, this book is based upon the premise that there are two fundamental requirements for life to have genuine meaning and purpose—the existence of the Divine and the possibility of immortality. In Part One, we will look at the three most common reasons why people reject the concept of God (or gods), which are: Science, Evolution, and Evil. Clearly these are deep topics and there have been enough volumes written about them to fill a small library. In no way am I attempting to exhaustively explore every "pro" and "con" argument surrounding them. Instead I am trying to demonstrate that there are valuable arguments that one should consider before flat out rejecting belief in the supernatural or a Higher Power—no matter what you call it.

In Part Two, we will look at the Christian narrative concerning the existence of God, the condition of mankind, and the possibility of immortality. It is my belief that the Christian perspective makes the most sense of the world around us. As the famous "once atheist" and renowned philosopher Anthony Flew stated,

> "As I have said more than once, no other religion enjoys anything like the combination of a charismatic figure like Jesus and a first-class intellectual like St. Paul. If you're wanting omnipotence to set up a religion, it seems to me this is the one to beat!"

It is my hope that you will see that your life does have genuine meaning and purpose because the Divine is real, immortality is available, and one of most important things you may ever do with your life is to consider Jesus.

Part One
The Case for the Divine

1

Religion or Jesus?

A number of years ago I decided to take an informal poll in order to honestly understand what people thought about Christianity, compared to what they thought about Jesus. When the setting was appropriate—such as in a restaurant where the waitress wasn't really busy, or on an airplane where I could have a quiet conversation with the passenger next to me—I would ask people a few simple questions and, with few exceptions, people were often very happy to help.

What I asked them first was: "Can you tell me what your opinion is of Christianity?" There were several Christians I polled who thought Christianity was wonderful; but there were even more people who had a negative impression of it. It came as no surprise that a number of them said something along the lines of, "I think Christians are narrow-minded," or, "Christians are hypocrites." People gave examples about Christians they knew who talked about love but acted hatefully, or they said that Christians are judgmental or closed-minded—along with other remarks that many Christians typically hear.

> **People don't seem to have a problem with Jesus, but they do have a problem with the people who are supposed to be following his example and his teachings.**

What I found interesting was that in almost every case, despite the fact that my question was, "What is your opinion of *Christianity*?" people described their impressions of *Christians* instead, and never actually spoke about Christianity itself.

This led me to my second question: "If that is your opinion of Christians, then what is your opinion of Jesus, who is the leader of Christianity?" Amazingly, most people gave me an entirely different response. I remember one woman in particular who said, "I like Jesus, I don't have a problem with him." On another occasion a woman overhearing the conversation spoke up and said, "Jesus was a cool guy, I like him—I just don't like Christians."

The pattern I saw emerge was that, for the most part, the people who had a problem with Christianity (and Christians in particular) didn't have a problem with Jesus—the person whose life and teachings Christianity is founded upon. Clearly there is a problem here—a major disconnect. People don't seem to have a problem with Jesus, but they do have a problem with the people who are supposed to be following his example and his teachings.

Jesus Didn't Come to Start a New Religion

Following Jesus' life and death, a new religion called Christianity eventually emerged. The "religion" of Christianity is what we see around us today, and it includes formal systems of creeds, ceremonies, traditions, and worship. The religion of Christianity is about churches, programs, and raising money. But I don't believe Jesus did what he did with the intention of starting a new religion. His intent was not only to bring love, peace, and forgiveness, but also something more important that is relational—the restoration of man's relationship with God as our Father.

Some Things Jesus Did and Didn't Say

If we really want to understand what Jesus' intentions were, we should look closely at what he said; and, perhaps just as crucial, we should consider what he didn't say. Here are some things Jesus *didn't* say...even though many people's actions seem to indicate that he did!

- "Come to me, all you who are weary and burdened, and I will give you a checklist of things to do and not do in order for God to love you."

- "If you love me, you will regularly attend a church."

- "Take my yoke upon you and learn to disparage all other religions and their followers, drug addicts, homosexuals, etc."

- "I have come to start a new religion."

- "My Father's house has a limited number of rooms, and I only give the room keys to special people. But no worries, there is plenty of room in Hell."

- "And you will know the truth, and the truth will make you superior to everyone else who thinks differently than you."

None of that sounds at all like the Jesus I know and follow! Yet this is exactly how many Christians behave with their "religion" of Christianity. Let's compare those statements with some of the things Jesus actually *did* say:

- "Come to me, all you who are weary and burdened, and I will give you rest." (Matt. 11:28)

- "If you love me, keep my commands." (John 14:15)

- "Take my yoke upon you and learn from me, for I am gentle and humble in heart, and you will find rest for your souls." (Matt. 11:28-29)

- "I have come that you may have life, and have it to the full." (John 10:10)

- "My Father's house has many rooms; if that were not so, would I have told you that I am going there to prepare a place for you?" (John, 14:2)

- "You will know the truth, and the truth will set you free." (John 8:32)

Consider Jesus
From my informal survey, I learned that a lot of people have had negative experiences with Christians and that they

don't think too highly of Christianity as a result. If this is true of you, then please consider that your experience was with people, not with Jesus.

Maybe you haven't wanted to learn about Jesus because you believe that all religions are basically the same; however, certainly they can't all be correct when they make conflicting claims. It seems reasonable that it is not the similarities we should be concerned with, but the differences.

Perhaps you have rejected the idea of God because you have trouble reconciling the idea of belief in a Creator with the evidence from science; or you may have trouble believing in a loving God when there is so much evil in the world. These are legitimate reasons people have for doubting Christianity, but I believe that there are sound

> **If the Jesus of the Bible isn't real, then I need to worship the person who created the character.**

and valid arguments for each one of them to dispel the doubt they cause.

I once heard someone say, "If the Jesus of the Bible isn't real, then I need to worship the person who created the character." His point was that what is written about Jesus makes him out to be a pretty remarkable guy. But Jesus isn't some fictional character, he is real; he was born, he lived and died, and the entire world was turned upside-down by his teachings and by his followers.

If you are open to considering that what you have seen, heard, or experienced about him isn't accurate, then please join me as we examine the arguments and evidences for why every person should "consider Jesus."

2

Having a Meaningful Life

A few years ago, I was sitting in the airport terminal waiting to board my flight. The purpose of my trip was not a happy one; I was flying from Indianapolis to California for the funeral of my daughter Sheila. My mind was flooded with thoughts and vivid memories of my precious girl, who had just lost a three-year battle with breast cancer at the young age of 31, leaving behind two beautiful little children.

As I watched people pass by—some hurrying toward their gates, others arriving from distant places—I wanted to shout to the world with every bit of air in my lungs, "My daughter just died!" As silly as it may have seemed, I wanted the world to stop for just one minute and acknowledge my little girl. As I thought about it, I realized that what I really wanted was to know that my daughter's life mattered.

My pain in the airport was still freshly imprinted on my mind as I stood at the podium in the chapel, in front of the friends and family who had come to acknowledge my daughter at her memorial. Sadness was painted across every face as I looked around the room. It was packed, with every seat taken, people lining the walls, and some even spilling out into the lobby. Scanning the crowd, I knew then that Sheila's life *did* matter. The evidence was in all people present—those whose lives she had touched.

> ... deep down, everyone wants to know that their life matters, that it has meaning and purpose.

We Need Our Lives to Matter

One of the lessons that my daughter's death taught me was that, deep down, everyone wants to know that their life matters, that it has meaning and purpose. One of the worst feelings a person can have is the sense of irrelevance, the feeling that they are not important and that their life is worthless. It's a terrible feeling, exacerbated by something inside of us which tells us that we need to matter, we need to have a purpose, our lives must have meaning.

Our inner need for purpose pushes all of us endlessly toward various endeavors. When we are young, we tend to focus on the things that will help to establish us firmly in our lives: getting an education, getting married, starting a family, beginning our careers and climbing the so-called ladder of success. The proverbial list of beauty, fame, fortune, and power is a driving force for many, but these are only the symptoms of our desire for genuine meaning, not the proof that we have achieved it.

A number of years ago, I read an account about Russian prisoners who were sent to the Gulags—work camps in the frozen wastelands of Siberia. Some of the men were assigned the task of digging a deep hole in the frozen tundra. They would toil hour after hour for days on end, and once the guard said the hole was large enough, they were ordered to fill it back up. Their days were consumed with meaningless physical labor. Lost in a sea of anonymity, doing work that was absolutely pointless, and lacking any means of measuring progress, the majority of the prisoners slowly went insane. The conclusion is: take away meaning and purpose from life, and you will lose the will to live. The reason for this is, as William Lane Craig states: "Man cannot live consistently and happily as though life ultimately were without value, meaning or purpose."[1]

Genuine Meaning

Throughout the ages, philosophers and sages have struggled to find the meaning of life. One of the biggest difficulties they face is that they can see that death is inevitable. It is the great equalizer that every person encounters, whether rich or poor, wise or foolish, strong or weak. The problem lies in that, if death causes everyone to pass out of existence, then ultimately, what meaning can there be to life? If this world is nothing more than what we see, say, and do, then death ultimately renders everything inconsequential.

---

1. William Lane Craig, *Reasonable Faith: Christian Truth and Apologetics* (Wheaton: Crossway, 2008), 84.

Some have attempted to get around this reality by saying that their lives are not meaningless if they have done good, made the world a better place, or influenced others in a positive way. Although this may help us to *feel* good about ourselves, if we pass out of existence when we die, then our lives are ultimately meaningless; and filling them with activities—no matter how noble they may seem—does nothing to change that. What is important is not that we have a *sense of meaning* for our lives, but that there is a *genuine reason* for living.

Two Viewpoints About the Physical World

Where did the physical world come from? What caused all that we see around us to come into being? How and why did life originate? And, what is it that allows us to even ponder our existence? These are some very profound questions that people throughout the ages have sought to answer. After much personal reflection, it seems to me that there are fundamentally only two possible answers: either everything in our world—

If this world is nothing more than what we see, say, and do, then death ultimately renders everything inconsequential.

including you and me—is an accident, the result of random actions; or it must be deliberate, the result of intentional forces. Let's consider those two possibilities and the implications of each position.

The Naturalist Position

Many people believe that the world was formed solely through natural processes; we call this position "naturalism" or "materialism," as in everything is dependent upon "matter." This is the belief that the entire physical world, the entire universe, is the product of matter, motion, chemistry, and physical forces interacting randomly. In other words, everything that we see around us is caused by mere accidental interactions. If this is the case, then by definition it means that nothing is directed; there is no intentionality. Those who truly believe this must also accept its necessary conclusion: that lacking intent can only mean there is no ultimate meaning to life. No matter how we may "feel," or even if we assign meaning to our lives, the honest conclusion of this viewpoint is that there is no meaning to any life, including yours - and that's a very disturbing realization to face.

The Deist Position

The alternative to the Naturalist position and its random-universe perspective is the belief that life is not an accident—there was a deliberate action at the formation of the physical world and the origin of all life, which implies there was an intent, a genuine purpose to our existence. Anything that would be powerful enough to *cause* the world is, by its very nature, larger than the physical world itself. It must supersede nature; that is, it must be "super-natural."

If we want a life with genuine meaning, we must accept that there is a cause-agent, which some have described as the Divine, a Higher Power, or God—an entity existing outside of our world that brought it into existence through deliberate actions and with specific intentions. Either this is true, or we must face the alternative that we are just accidental products of matter colliding together. William Lane Craig succinctly summarized this thought:

> "Modern man thought that when he had gotten rid of God, he had freed himself from all that repressed and stifled him. Instead, he discovered that in killing God, he had only succeeded in orphaning himself. For if there is no God, then man's life becomes absurd."[2]

---

2. Ibid., 71.

The first condition that must be met, if this world is to have any genuine meaning or purpose, is that God must exist. If He does not, then both man and the universe are merely accidents of random actions and processes. Inspired by Francis Schaeffer, William Lane Craig warns, "Once God is denied, human life becomes worthless...."[3]

Life and Death—and Life Beyond Death

I understand that you may not believe that God exists, but let's just assume for a moment that He does. Does the mere existence of God automatically equate to life having genuine purpose and meaning, in the sense of there being an enduring or lasting significance? I don't think so. I believe that even if God does exist, there must be one more essential factor in place in order for our lives to have *genuine* meaning: we must be able to attain immortality...a way to exist beyond the grave.

> **In order for life to have meaning, the only logical conclusion is that both God and the possibility of immortality must exist.**

How can anyone say that there is any real meaning or purpose for this life if it ends in a big fat zero—an empty void of nothing?

If we cease to exist at the time of our death, then no matter how much meaning we ascribe to our lives, in the end it becomes nothing. Even if we changed the world, altered history in a positive way, and greatly influenced others around us, if our life ended with our last breath, then how could there be any real meaning? After all, we did nothing more than influence other finite lives, lives that are also ending in nothingness—lives that are all equally meaningless. It would be like cleaning the furniture on the Titanic as it sank into the

---

3. Ibid., 70.

frozen deep. It's futile! In order for life to have meaning, the only logical conclusion is that both God and the possibility of immortality must exist.

Eternity in the Hearts

I have been with many people who were on their deathbeds, and the one consistent thing that I have seen is how tenaciously they cling to life. Even people who have had no belief in God or the supernatural still fight for life until their last breath because, deep down, they know it is better to be alive than to be dead. We all strive to live each day as if there is a purpose to living, and we all seek meaning for our lives. Thousands of years ago, a king named Solomon wrote that God has set eternity in the heart of man (Eccl. 3:11). Perhaps he was referring to this desire within us.

There is nothing wrong with having doubts concerning the existence of God and immortality. If you are someone who does not accept that God exists, I hope that you will keep an open mind during the next few chapters as we explore some of the most common reasons why people reject the existence of God.

3

Worldviews: We All Have
One... What's Yours?

The last time I checked, I had a belly button—and I bet you do, too! Of course you do, everyone does; and, like a belly button, everyone has a worldview. The topic of worldviews has become philosophically popular over the past several years. When we speak of a worldview, we are not talking about what the earth looks like from the window of the International Space Station. A worldview is not a physical view; it describes the internalized belief system that each person holds. Your worldview affects how you think, feel, and interact with the world around you.

Your Worldview is Your Window to the World

We come from the womb with a mind that, apart from the most basic of survival instincts, is in many ways like a blank schoolroom chalkboard. Very quickly, we begin to write our experiences on the slate of our mind and those experiences form our perceptions. The first things we write are usually concepts such as, "the world is a safe place, or not," or, "I can trust my needs to be taken care of, or not." These thoughts begin to form the most basic part of our worldview. They are our internalized beliefs about the world around us; thus, the most fundamental aspects of our worldview are not beliefs that we have consciously decided to embrace. As Phillip E. Johnson concisely states in the foreword of the book, *Total Truth*:

> **We do not ordinarily see our own worldview, but we see everything else by looking through it.**

> "Understanding worldviews is a bit like trying to see the lens of one's own eye. We do not ordinarily see our own worldview, but we see everything else by looking through it. Simply put, our worldview is the window by which we view the world, and decide, often subconsciously, what is real and important, or unreal and unimportant."[1]

Our Worldviews Shift and Change

A worldview is not a jumbled mess of disconnected

---

1. Nancy R. Pearcey, *Total Truth: Liberating Christianity from its Cultural Captivity* (Wheaton: Crossway, 2004), 11.

thoughts, nor is it a formalized philosophy. It is a pattern of thinking that produces biases, likes, dislikes, and core beliefs, and it isn't static; it can and does change over time. As we grow older, our worldviews continue to be shaped through questioning, analyzing, and reviewing the world and those in it. Returning to the chalkboard analogy above, worldviews become the surface where equations are reviewed, erased, and rewritten. We can even change things that we once understood to be absolutes.

Fords, Chevrolets, and Worldviews

When I was growing up, my dad and most of his friends had Chevrolet cars and trucks. I would occasionally hear them good-naturedly poke jabs at other brands: "Chryslers are junk, and Ford (F.O.R.D) stands for Fix Or Repair Daily." Of course, this was only an opinion...but because I was exposed to it, it conditioned my worldview. I developed a bias towards Chevy and against other vehicle brands. As time went on (and my worldview went largely unchallenged), I became even more inclined to purchase Chevys, and when I saw other brands on the road, I tended to think less of the cars—and the drivers—all because of the fraction of my worldview that favored Chevys over every other vehicle brand. In some way, everyone carries a mental model of the universe that tells them what the world is like and how they should relate to it.[2]

> As we grow older, our worldviews continue to be shaped through questioning, analyzing, and reviewing the world and those in it.

Worldviews and the Deeper Questions of Life

Although the example about cars is a simple illustration,

---

2. Ibid., 23.

it accurately depicts how worldviews work. Your worldview affects almost everything about how you perceive the world around you; for instance, whether you prefer colder or warmer climates, are more inclined toward conservative or liberal thinking, whether you tend more to trust or distrust people, whether you view the world as generally bad or good, etc. We even rely on our worldview to answer some of life's most fundamental questions: Does God exist? Is there life after death? What is the meaning of life? Does life have a real purpose?

Let's consider the following scenario. Before you go to bed, you decide to watch a television show in which the cast is searching for evidence of Bigfoot. The next morning, you read a story in the newspaper about a man who was arrested for assisting his wife in committing suicide because she was suffering from a terminal illness. On your way to work, you hear a report on the radio where a person claims to have seen a UFO. And then when you arrive at your job a coworker tells you that she thinks she's been contacted by a loved one who died a few years ago.

While this series of events may seem disjointed, each occurrence has something in common: how you receive and react to it. The way in which you interpret everything you saw, read, and heard in the scenario above is based on your worldview—whether you respond with skepticism, excitement, chagrin, or any other of a myriad of emotions. It is all dependent on your worldview because your worldview shapes, informs, and determines how you define everything around you and all of your experiences—even friendship, love, and loyalty. Your worldview also impacts your views regarding mortality, life, death, the universe, and the supernatural. Although everyone has a worldview, that does not mean they are equal, nor are they neutral—as in, without consequence.

Our Worldview Has Real Consequences

The worldview we hold actually has life-or-death consequences. For instance, "Do you believe a higher power exists, such as God?" How you answer that question is the result of your worldview. And if you do believe in a force such as God, do you think that He is kind or cruel, good or bad? Is it possible to even know God? Is there more than one God? If you have rejected the concept of a "higher power," that, too, is based on your worldview.

A conversation I once had with a friend turned to the subject of ISIS, the radical Islamic group responsible for the deaths of many innocent

> **Clearly, worldviews can and do have life-or-death-consequences.**

people around the world largely due to religious differences. During the conversation, my friend said, "I don't understand what the problem is...don't we all worship the same God?" Her viewpoint that all religions are worshipping the same deity was the result of her worldview, and whether true or not, ISIS would definitely have disagreed with her. Their actions indicated that they didn't believe we all worship the same God—they had a different worldview. Clearly, worldviews can and do have life-or-death consequences.

Seeking the Best Explanation

The beliefs we hold are frequently in conflict with the beliefs of others. In such cases, it is right to ask, "How do I know who is correct?"

> **Conclusive, inescapable evidence is not necessary for us to rightly accept something as true or false.**

Wouldn't it be great if we could have evidence that proves what belief is 100% correct? It sure would solve a lot of disagreements, but most people understand that this is an unrealistic expectation. In fact, not even science bases its conclusions on having 100% proof to determine whether a matter is true or false. Instead, we all form beliefs on the basis of probabilities.

Conclusive, inescapable evidence is not necessary for us to rightly accept something as true or false. Instead, what we should be looking for is the *best explanation* of the evidence at hand. The best evidence scenario is what we base our everyday decision-making and subsequent actions upon. Two clear and obvious examples of this are found in the fields of medicine and law enforcement.

When I see a physician for an ailment, he examines me, considers all the symptoms and the results of various tests, and then renders a diagnosis based on the greatest likelihood—the highest probability—of what I am suffering from. This is his *best explanation.* Oftentimes he cannot have absolute, 100% certainty of what ails me, which is why people with serious diagnoses are frequently encouraged to seek more than one doctor's *opinion.*

Law enforcement also relies on this "highest-probability scenario" to conduct the arrest and prosecution of criminals. They examine the crime scene, take witness statements, and make a determination of what they believe took place based on the *best explanation* of the evidence. When it comes to making worldview decisions, we too must look for the greatest probability—not irrefutable, 100% proof, but what conclusion is best supported by the evidence at hand. With this in mind, let's examine two fundamental worldviews, the Natural and the Supernatural, to determine which one produces the best explanation of the world we live in.

The Natural Worldview

The Natural worldview, as mentioned in Chapter 2, holds that everything we see is the result of matter, motion, chemistry, and electromagnetism in random interactions. It postulates that there is no truth beyond the physical world, or any genuine meaning or purpose to life beyond random and accidental interactions of matter. Naturalism is also referred to as Materialism because it asserts that matter is the only reality, there is no spiritual realm, and that God does not exist. It even promotes that emotions, values, ethics and other non-physical matters exist only in the realm of the subjective and cannot be trusted or considered true.

The problem many people have experienced with Naturalism is that it does not seem to adequately explain many of the realities of life. To borrow a phrase from Nancy Pearcey, the Naturalist has a "worldview built on a foundation that will always be partial, incomplete, one-sided, and off-balance."[3] It is as if Naturalism is a box that is simply too small to fit the reality of the world inside it. The world has too many "anomalies" that Naturalism simply cannot adequately explain.

We intuitively sense that there is more to life than the mere physical realm, and that people are more than just biological creatures; we all experience emotions such as love and hate, and morality seems to be more than merely a construct of the human mind. The fact that we all make deliberate choices and exercise free will shows us that life is not just the result of random events. We also deeply perceive that life is better than death and many accept that there is evidence for a spiritual

---

3. Nancy Pearcey, *Saving Leonardo: A Call to Resist the Secular Assault on Mind, Morals & Meaning* (Nashville: B&H Publishing, 2010), 244.

realm. These are all things that do not fit within the box of Naturalism, which is why, although it was very popular at one time, Naturalism has given way to more and more people adopting some form of a Supernatural worldview.

The Supernatural Worldview

The Supernatural worldview includes elements of Materialism, and adds to it a spiritual outlook. This perspective takes into account that there is more to reality than just the physical world, and it accepts that a supernatural, or spiritual realm, also exists.

There are a number of Supernatural worldviews. The two main forms are Deism and Theism. Deists believe that a higher power exists in some form, but they tend to regard it as unknowable and impersonal. Theists go a step further, with most believing in a particular God, or gods. There are many forms of theism, such as monotheists, who believe there is one God; polytheists, who believe there are many gods; and even pantheists, who believe God/god is part of everything. These various Supernatural worldviews include beliefs in a Creator, life after death, and that the world and all life has a purpose.

To a Supernaturalist, Naturalism does not properly account for or sufficiently explain the world in which we live. One area in particular that it does not adequately address for the Supernaturalist is the matter of morality. If, as the Naturalist believes, life truly ends at the grave, then how does one explain the human drive to seek the moral high ground? It would seem that if the Naturalist explanation is true, life is too short for anything other than self-interest. What would be the benefit of doing selfless acts and living like a saint rather than being completely self-focused? People often adopt a Supernatural and Theistic worldview because of the high value it places on life.

We Need to Look at the Whole Picture, Not Just a Part

While the Naturalist viewpoint may seem to have reasonable explanations for many physical realities, it still falls short because it doesn't look at the whole picture. It's like describing a computer system based solely on the "hardware," while ignoring the "software" that directs and runs that hardware. We can examine and explain all the physical realities of a DVD, but the disc is more than just its physical properties. It carries information in the form of a code—a binary computer language—embedded on the surface layer of the disc.

Similarly, biological DNA, the basic building blocks of all living entities, is a physical, structured arrangement of amino acids, but it also contains a type of "software"— coded messages that instruct it on what proteins to build, and how. We can explain its structure and even determine the composition of its chemical components, but we can't explain the information that the DNA strand communicates. This holds true for the DNA in all living entities, whether they be plants, simple celled organisms, or complex higher life forms. Naturalism can look at the biological structures and interconnections between species, but it does not adequately explain matters that exist beyond the physical realm.

We want to make sure that the worldview we hold does not just look at part of the world, but rather at its entirety, and that the box of our worldview doesn't have things poking out—parts of reality that it does not address, and/or denies. We must examine our worldview and seek to adopt one that provides the best explanation, because what's really at stake in the battle of the worldviews is whether life is genuinely meaningful or not.

Let's Examine the Evidence

The evidence of realities beyond the physical realm is compelling enough to warrant deeper scrutiny. No matter what position we finally decide on, whether Naturalist or Supernaturalist, if we take the time to reflect, analyze, and critique each of them, we can then honestly say we have chosen based upon the "best evidence." To quote Nancy Pearcey once again:

> "Yet to define what is rational solely by whether it fits your worldview is an invalid move because it rules out all other truth claims by definition. You do not even have to investigate the evidence. A serious search for truth does not start by stacking the deck."[4]

In the following chapters, we will explore the three most common reasons people cite for their rejection of God, what many claim as irreconcilable conflicts between: 1) God and science, 2) God and evolution, and 3) God and evil. If life truly ends at the grave, then we have nothing to lose. But if there is any chance that it doesn't—if there is a possibility for immortality—then what is stopping us from searching out the matter and embracing the best conclusion based on the evidence. As the famous mathematician, physicist, and philosopher Blaise Pascal once indicated about the wager of whether God exists or not, "We have nothing to lose, and infinite to gain."

---

4. Nancy Pearcey, *Finding Truth, 5 Principles for Unmasking Atheism, Secularism, and other God Substitutes,* (Colorado Springs: David Cook, 2015), 74.

4

God and Science

One of the reasons people commonly cite for their rejection of a Supernaturalist worldview is that they have difficulty reconciling science with belief in God. On the one hand, it is easy to understand why: traditionally, most people see science as infallible, objective, and provable. It is considered to be trustworthy, dealing in hard facts, and is thought to be "good," because it is logical and rational. Its domain deals in subjects that are tangible, real, and "true," because it deals in matters that can be measured, weighed, observed, and repeatedly verified.

God, on the other hand, is in the realm of religion, which many believe to be full of myths and matters of opinion, even speculation. Some surmise that because God cannot be observed or measured, He cannot be proven to exist. Many people also believe that religion and its adherents actually stunt scientific exploration—that those who believe in God are stuck, unmoving, closed-minded, and antiquated. And there are others who hold the position that science has actually proven religion to be wrong.

Clearly, if viewed as described above, science and religion are opposed. It is true that there have been times when religion has hindered scientific discovery; there have also been times when religious beliefs were ultimately proven by science to be false. But it is also true that many positions in science have also been proven to be wrong.

Why Do We Believe Science and Religion are Opposed?

One of the reasons that science and matters of faith seem to be opposed is because over time people have split them into two different, mutually exclusive categories. As indicated previously, people these days consider science to be factual; it is defined as *objective*, based on facts rather than feelings or opinions, whereas matters of faith are considered to be in the realm of the *subjective*, that which is "subject" to one's perspective, opinions, or feelings. By splitting science and religion in this fashion, we've created a dualistic form of thinking that pits the two against each other.

This dualism even carries over into how people interact with each other. In the public arena, it is perfectly acceptable to discuss any factual matters such as the weather, a job, a car, sports, family, etc. On the other hand, matters of faith and religion are considered to be one's opinion and are reserved for the private arena. However, unlike today, there was a time when the natural and supernatural domains were understood to be part of a singular whole—two intertwined realities, both of them equally true.

At one time, things such as morality, values, and ethics were thought to be as true as any scientific empirical results. Problems arose when many people became so impressed with the accomplishments of the sciences that they began to think of them as the sole source of truth. This shifting of focus from the entwined view of science and faith is summarized well by Nancy Pearcey in her book, *Saving Leonardo*:

> *...if science is true, and religion, or a belief in the supernatural, is also true, then the very nature of truth necessitates that they must harmonize.*

"Empiricism is the doctrine that all knowledge is derived from the senses—what we see, hear, hold, weigh, and measure. Obviously, moral truths cannot be stuffed into a test tube or studied under a microscope. As a result, moral truths were no longer considered truths at all, but merely expressions of emotion."[1]

Thus began the fracturing of truth from a singular reality, once comprised of both the natural and supernatural, into the two opposing views of "facts" versus "values"—facts being real, and values (which includes all religious beliefs) being nothing more than human mental constructs and personal opinions.

---

1. Nancy Pearcey, *Saving Leonardo*, 24.

Must Science and Religion be Opposed to Each Other?

People have been conditioned to believe that it is the nature of science and religion to oppose each other. But that view does not seem necessarily true—primarily because if science is true, and religion, or a belief in the supernatural, is also true, then the very nature of truth necessitates that they must harmonize. The two cannot contradict one another—truth must always agree with truth.

> Many people have no idea that the greatest scientific minds of past generations were Theists.

In order to resolve the apparent conflict between God and science, there are four basic questions that we should answer:

1. Is it the very nature of science and faith (religion) to be at war? Must they be in conflict with each other?

2. Does it follow that a scientifically-minded person has to avoid religious beliefs?

3. Is there a different way to view the relationship between the spiritual and the scientific? Must the spiritual be at odds with the natural?

4. Is there any scientific evidence that points toward, or away from, the existence of God?

Must Science and Religion be in Conflict with Each Other?

Although it is true that many of the biggest names in science nowadays are atheists, this hasn't always been the case. Many people have no idea that the greatest scientific minds of past generations were Theists. In fact, most of the founders of the various scientific disciplines were religious men and women who had worldviews that were thoroughly integrated with their belief in and practice of science. Consider some of the following examples of great scientific minds who were also very devout Supernaturalists:

Nicolaus Copernicus (1473-1543)—A Polish astronomer who demonstrated mathematically that the sun is the center of the solar system and that planets travel around the sun (heliocentrism). The previous model, developed by Ptolemy, had the earth at the center of the solar system. Copernicus' model began a scientific revolution, with many even thinking of him as the father of modern astronomy.

Sir Francis Bacon (1561-1627)—An Englishman credited with establishing the scientific method of study based upon inquiry, experimentation, and inductive reasoning. The methodology he developed is still adhered to and followed by scientists to the present day.

Sir Isaac Newton (1643-1727)—Although many merely equate his name with apples and gravity, Newton is considered to be the greatest mathematician ever known. He was directly involved with the development of calculus (the mathematical analysis of curves and change), and the fundamental theory of optics (he also built the first reflecting telescope); a theory on light wavelength, refraction, and diffraction using prisms and thin sheets of glass; the theory of sound propagation; as well as other fundamental laws of physics. As brilliant as he was in the sciences, most don't realize that he actually spent even more of his time studying theology.

Blaise Pascal (1632-1662)—A mathematician, physicist, inventor, writer, and philosopher, he is known for laying the foundation for today's probability theory. He realized that events don't just happen randomly, but that they rely upon what directly preceded them. He also made discoveries in atmospheric pressure and developed an early form of a calculator—the precursor to the modern computer. He also authored many theological writings in which he gave defenses of the Christian faith.

Michael Faraday (1791-1867)—Known today as the Father of Electricity, he discovered electromagnetic induction, the principle that voltage is induced in a changing magnetic field. This is the basis for all electric generators. He also discovered the concept of harnessing electrical fields both inside and outside of a cage, known today as a Faraday Cage. This concept is used for the protection of electrical equipment, especially from electromagnetic pulses. Even our modern televisions and microwave ovens rely upon this concept in order to work.

Does it Follow that a Scientifically Minded Person has to Avoid Religious Beliefs?

Clearly, the historical record shows that a scientifically-minded person does not need to avoid a spiritual worldview or religious beliefs. Science and religion do not need to be opposed—in fact, the evidence shows that most of the greatest scientific breakthroughs and discoveries ever made were by people who held a belief in a Creator, a Designer, who was behind the physical world we see around us. The view that science and God must be opposed to each other is simply not true.

Is There a Different Way to View the Relationship Between the Spiritual and the Scientific?

Having a supernatural worldview, or even a Theistic one, does not in any way need to inhibit our quest for scientific discovery. When we open the door to a supernatural worldview, we create the possibility for science to demonstrate, not only how things work, but also to reveal possible evidence of a creative intelligence behind the creation. Science then can become a forensic tool used to uncover the fingerprints of a Creator.

Consider the following scientific disciplines:

Cosmology—the origin and structure of the universe
Astronomy—the stars, planets and outer space
Zoology—animals and their behavior
Biology—living things and the processes that occur in them
Anatomy—the structure of living things
Geology—rocks, soil, land formation and the Earth
Paleontology—fossils and dinosaurs
Genetics—how genes control the characteristics of plants, animals, and people
Anthropology—human races, origins, societies and cultures

And much, much more…

A scientist with a Naturalist worldview approaches the abovementioned disciplines from the perspective that all of these things are the result of purely random and accidental processes. But a scientist who allows for the Supernaturalist worldview approaches these matters from the perspective that what we see is intentional, purposeful, and indicative of a Designer behind it all. Anthony Flew, the famous philosopher and former renowned atheist, put it well: "He who knows nature knows God, but not because God is nature, but because the pursuit of science in studying nature leads to religion."[2]

Is There Any Scientific Evidence that Points Toward, or Away from, the Existence of God?

One of the things that physics has uncovered is that there are constraints built into the very fabric of the world. These are called physical constants, and they are believed to be universal in both quantity and time. The very structure of all matter, from vast galaxies down to subatomic particles, is governed by these limits.

One of these constants is the speed of light, which has been measured at 299,792,458 meters per second (as measured in a vacuum—meaning there is nothing to interfere with its movement). The reason light speed is called a fundamental constant is because no matter where one goes in the universe, the speed of light is always the same. This is also true of many other physical properties, including the force of gravity, various properties of electromagnetism, and the relationship between mass and energy. Like the speed of light, each one has a constant property that exists within a very narrow range of values.

A Finely Tuned World

In an attempt to describe how delicate and precise these properties are, it has been said that the universe is very "finely tuned." Imagine walking into the most sophisticated control room that has ever existed, a room filled with hundreds of dials each directly correlating to a fundamental physical constant. One knob controls the speed of light, another the force of gravity,

---

2. Anthony Flew, PhD., *There is A God: How the World's Most Notorious Atheist Changed His Mind,* (New York: Harper Collins, 2007), 101.

another the mass of an electron, and so on. Each knob is so finely tuned that the slightest adjustment would result in utter calamity throughout the entire physical world. If you moved the gravity knob ever-so-slightly, increasing its strength, all the stars would collapse in on themselves. Moving the knob in the other direction, decreasing the force of gravity, would result in the disintegration of the stars, since there would no longer be enough force to maintain their form. Slightly adjusting any of the knobs in any direction would bring about catastrophe, causing all life to cease. This is why the universe is said to be "finely tuned."

The questions that we must ask ourselves are these:

1. Does the universe and its scientifically-verified fundamental constants point to randomness or to intentionality?

2. Is this merely an accident, the result of chance interactions?

3. Although one may be able to say that things happen by chance all the time, do chance and accidents cause the very nucleus of an atom to hold together?

The narrow band of values in which all the fundamental constants interact points clearly to intentionality. Flew, recognizing the fundamental "Laws of Nature" and these constants, states:

"Virtually no major scientist today claims that the fine tuning was purely a result of chance factors at work in a single universe...fine tuning is best explained by divine design."[3]

---

3. Ibid, 115.

The reason why Flew modifies the above statement with the caveat "single universe" is because he acknowledges the scientific postulation of a "multiverse" theory, which suggests that there could be trillions of parallel universes. The premise is that with many universes, some could be operating according to different laws and physical constraints. While we can postulate about anything, including the existence of trillions of universes, the fact

> **What we must ask ourselves is, "Why is there something instead of nothing?" - a "something" that is bound by constraints, physical constants, and the Laws of Nature?**

remains that there is absolutely no evidence for more than the one universe in which we live. The multiverse theory is nothing more than speculation—fictional thinking—and this is not a viable explanation for the finely-tuned universe around us.

> "The important point is not merely that there are regularities in nature, but these regularities are mathematically precise, universal, and 'tied together'. Einstein spoke of them as 'reason incarnate.' The question we should ask is how nature came packaged in this fashion? This is certainly the question scientists from Newton to Einstein to Heisenberg have asked— and answered. Their answer was the Mind of God."[4]

Does the Big Bang Really Explain Things Adequately?

What we must ask ourselves is, "Why is there *something* instead of *nothing?*"—a "something" that is bound by constraints, physical constants, and the Laws of Nature?

---

4. Ibid, 96.

According to some scientists, the cosmological evidence indicates that everything in the universe began in an instant of time, which they refer to as the "Big Bang," when all energy was densely compacted, and then, in a single moment, suddenly exploded, rapidly expanding and producing all physical matter. The result is the fathomless universe we see around us. The scientific evidence does seem to support a time when all energy and matter expanded from a singular point, which according to a theistic perspective is the moment of creation. Conversely, the Big Bang falls far short of answering why there is *something* instead of *nothing*.

> **Science has taken us to the First Event, but it can't take us further to the First Cause.**

"Over the centuries, thinkers who have considered the concepts of "nothing" have been careful to point out that "nothing" is not a kind of something. Absolute nothingness means no laws, no vacuums, no fields, no energy, no structures, no physical or mental entities of any kind…It has no properties or potentialities. Absolute nothingness cannot produce something given endless time—in fact, there can be no time in absolute nothingness."[5]

The Big Bang Leads Us to God

In 1985, Allan Rex Sandage, the protégé of Edwin Hubble, took the stage at The Conference of Science and Religion in Oxford, England. Few scientists at the time were as highly regarded as Mr. Sandage in the field of cosmology. Publically known to be an atheist, he shocked the audience when he stated:

---

5. Abraham Varghese, *There is A God; Appendix A: The "New Atheism:" A Critical Appraisal of Dawkins, Dennett, Wolpert, Harris, and Stenger"* (New York: Harper Collins, 2007), 170.

"The Big Bang was a supernatural event that cannot be explained within the realm of physics as we know it. Science has taken us to the First Event, but it can't take us further to the First Cause. The sudden emergence of matter, space, time, and energy points to the need for some kind of transcendence [i.e., God]."[6]

Speaking to a reporter, he was later quoted as saying:

"It was my science that drove me to the conclusion that the world is much more complicated than can be explained by science. It was only through the supernatural that I can understand the mystery of existence."[7]

There is a very fundamental principle of physics called "cause and effect." According to this principle, you cannot make something from nothing. There must be an initial cause behind the effect. Therefore, there must be something that caused the Big Bang.

Science is a wonderful thing, but it is only a tool. Much like a telescope or a microscope, we can use it to look at and discover the properties of the universe and the physical world around us, but it can only take us so far. There is a limit to what science can explain. Professor Stephen C. Meyer captured this well:

"If it is true there's a beginning to the universe, as modern cosmologists now agree, then this implies

6. Lee Strobel, *The Case for the Creator* (Grand Rapids: Zondervan, 2004), 84.
7. Ibid., 84.

a cause that transcends the universe. If the laws of physics are fine-tuned to permit life, as contemporary physicists are discovering, then perhaps there is a designer who fine-tuned them. If there's information in the cell, as molecular biology shows, then this suggests intelligent design. To get life going in the first place would have required biological information; the implications point beyond the material realm to a prior intelligent cause."[8]

Naturalism Doesn't Seem to Have All the Answers

Naturalism is limited in its ability to explain the physical realities of our world. Science alone cannot provide us with all the answers because there is a supernatural agent at work. Naturalism leaves us in a world devoid of meaning and purpose, whereas Supernaturalism provides us with answers and meaning; Supernaturalism offers the best explanation of the evidence we have.

If I am walking down the beach and come across the words "Bob loves Mary" in the sand at the water's edge, I would never think to myself, "How amazing that the waves created letters, and the letters have even formed words that communicate a particular meaning." Instead, I would immediately know that they were written by someone who had preceded me down the beach, because these letters point to intelligence because they communicate a message—they reveal meaning. When we see intelligent design, such as the words left on the beach, we know there is an Intelligent Designer.

> ...when we see all the evidence of design around us, we can rightly surmise that there must be a Designer...

8. Ibid., 89.

Similarly, when I see a painting hanging on a wall, or a beautiful sculpture carved of stone, I know there is a painter or sculptor responsible for creating it. No one visiting Mt. Rushmore, upon seeing the four Presidential faces carved in granite high up the mountainside would ever think that those were merely the product of the forces of nature. An explorer hacking through the jungle knows immediately when he has stumbled across the remains of a lost civilization, because he sees the evidence of design in the ruins. In the same way, when we see all the evidence of design around us, we can rightly surmise that there must be a Designer, an Intelligence behind it all.

There is no need to reject belief in the supernatural, or even a Creator, on the basis of science. Science is not opposed to the supernatural. Instead, when the science is viewed alongside the supernatural, it opens the door to greater understanding. For the Theist, science is much more than unraveling the mysteries of the physical universe. Like someone's fingerprints or DNA left behind at a crime scene which points in the direction of the perpetrator, science can help point us in the direction of the Creator.

If we genuinely follow the evidence, no matter where it leads, we will discover that it unmistakably points us to God. Albert Einstein, one of the most brilliant scientific minds of all time, once stated:

> "Every one who is seriously involved in the pursuit of science becomes convinced that a spirit is manifest in the laws of the Universe—a spirit vastly superior to that of man, and one in the face of which we with our modest powers must feel humble.[9]

9. http://www.simpletoremember.com/articles/a/einstein. Accessed 11/11/15.

5

God and Evolution

When I was in school, I was taught about Darwin and the Theory of Evolution—the theory that all life is the result of simple forms evolving into more complex ones over long periods of time. The theory had been around for quite some time, having been originally published in the 1860's, and it was only somewhat controversial when I was taught it in High School. Although some considered it to be only a theory, nowadays most people speak of evolution as if it has been unmistakably proven true.

Perusing any current biology or zoology textbook will reveal Darwinian Evolution as the very foundation that it rests upon.[1] It is virtually impossible to pick up any book dealing with the biological sciences and not find some evolutionary references in it. Some books point to the Evolutionary Tree of Life—a flow chart of sorts that depicts life emerging from the primordial soup of ancient earth and progressing to the complex life forms of the present day. Others make references to common features between species, or "remnant body parts," such as fetuses having vestiges of gills, a tail, and a yolk sac—in spite of the fact that these body parts are not actually gills, tails, or other features as described. There is little doubt about it: Darwin and his evolutionary theory have had a huge impact on the way people view the world today.

What is Darwinian Evolution?

As embedded as evolutionary thought has become, there still seems to be a lot of misunderstanding about what Darwinian evolution really is. Some of the confusion occurs because the word *evolution* has come to simply mean "to change." But when speaking of Darwinian Evolution, we are not merely referring to the changes that we commonly observe occurring within any given species. So before we explore the topic of evolution and God, let's eliminate the possibility of confusion and be clear on exactly what we are talking about when we say "Darwinian Evolution."

After closely observing how birds and animals physically adapt to their environments, Darwin proposed that these adaptations were the result of random genetic mutations

---

1. The author acknowledges that the modern use of the word "evolution" in biology was only used one time in print by Darwin in the closing paragraph of "The Origin of Species." The term "Darwinian Evolution" is used in the sense that Darwin is the primary source of the modern Theory of Evolution.

occurring over long periods of time. These changes were part of a mechanism that he labeled "evolution." He theorized that if these mutations proved to be beneficial for its survival, then the organism would pass those traits on to its offspring through "survival of the fittest." This process of gaining genetic mutations advantageous to an organism's survival is known as "natural selection." It was thought that, given enough time—such as thousands or millions of generations—the accumulation of various genetic changes could produce an entirely new species of creatures. Thus, the theory of evolution suggests that when enough mutations occur, a fish could slowly morph into an amphibian, then amphibians into reptiles, then reptiles into birds, and so on.

> **When Darwin proposed his theory of evolution, DNA and the role of genetics was not clearly understood.**

Darwinian Evolution teaches that all life started as very simple-celled organisms and that, over millions of years, many mutations randomly occurred which transformed the simple-celled organisms into all of the complex life forms we see around us today. In essence, it is the belief that all higher species descended from lower species, and that this process was "undirected" and the result of accidental but beneficial mutations.

Adaptation is Not Evolution

Darwin was an astute observer of the natural world around him, and, on the surface, his theory seems to make a lot of sense. A cornerstone of Darwin's proposition was that simple life forms led to more complex ones—the small led to the bigger, and the imperfect to the more perfect.[2] However, the

2. Vance Ferrell, *The Evolution Handbook* (Altamant: Evolution

variations and *adaptive changes* he noted were not the result of biological *mutatio*n or transformations into new species; they were the result of the vast genetic information already present in the DNA codes of the various species being expressed in different ways. This was not evolution as Darwin proposed, because no matter how diverse the offspring were, the dogs were still dogs, and the cats were still cats.

When Darwin proposed his theory of evolution, DNA and the role of genetics was not clearly understood. Then in the 1800's, Gregor Mendel discovered that genes carry both recessive and dominant traits. For instance, a person with blue eyes may also carry a trait for brown eyes, which is why two blue-eyed parents may actually produce a child with brown eyes, or vice versa.

Many people mistakenly refer to the adaptive changes we commonly see in the various species as evidence of Darwinian Evolution, but this is actually the result of the vast information already contained within the DNA. Within any given species there can be a tremendous amount of diversity. For instance, within the domestic dog species (Canus lupus familiaris) we find the tiny teacup Chihuahua as well as the large Great Dane. The diversity can be the result of the genetic mutations, but it can also be the result of the recombination of the dominant and recessive material already present in the genes.

> **Darwin was also aware that his theory had serious vulnerabilities which, if expanded upon, would prove it false.**

As Ralph Muncaster stated: "Sometimes a favorable trait is so advantageous that it helps animals survive while those

Facts Inc., 2002), 369-89.

without it die."[3] Dogs in the arctic whose genes produce thicker fur and other cold weather survival traits have a greater propensity to survive. As they survive, they will produce new offspring that will exhibit those same survival traits, while the dogs that are less adapted to that harsh environment will die off. This is adaptation, not evolution.

Evolution's Weaknesses

Even Darwin himself recognized the vast diversity of life in the world and doubted whether it was possible that such complexities and differences in all living organisms could evolve slowly from a single common ancestor. His basic assertion was that "natural selection can act only by taking advantage of slight successive variations; it can never take a leap, but must advance by the shortest and slowest steps."[4] Darwin was also aware that his theory had serious vulnerabilities which, if expanded upon, would prove it false. For example, if fossil evidence for "intermediate forms" was not found, it had to mean that there was no dynamic method in play to cause new speciation. Evolution also required that all anatomical structures and physiological systems had to be the result of gradual mutational changes over long periods of time. Therefore, one serious blow to his theory would be any evidence demonstrating biological features that did not slowly develop over time. As Darwin stated:

> "If it could be demonstrated that any complex organ existed which could not possibly have been formed by numerous successive, slight modifications, **my theory would absolutely break down**" (emphasis added).[5]

---

3. Ralph O. Muncaster, *Examine the Evidence: Creation Vs. Evolution* (Eugene: Harvest House, 2000), 8.

4. Charles Darwin, *On the Origin of Species by Means of Natural Selection, or the Preservation of Favoured Races in the Struggle for Life* (London: John Murray, 1859), 194.

5. Darwin, *On the Origin of Species*, (New York, NY: Bantam Dell,

Furthermore, in his book *On the Origin of Species*, Darwin strikingly admitted that there are many organs and features of animals that are too intricate and complex to have arisen from genetic mutations alone. He says,

> "To suppose that the eye with all its inimitable contrivances for adjusting the focus to different distances, for admitting different amounts of light, and for the correction of spherical and chromatic aberration, could have been formed by natural selection, seems, I freely confess, absurd in the highest degree."[6]

Icons of Evolution

Students around the world have been taught the concept of evolutionary theory using references to a number of traditional, albeit iconic, examples. There are several that are routinely cited, and although they have been proven false over time, they continue to be held as truth in the minds of many. We will explore the four most common icons, listed below:

- Stanley Miller experiment on the origins of life[7]
- Tree of Life diagram
- Ernst Haeckel's drawings of embryos
- Missing link

The Stanley Miller Experiment

One of the biggest difficulties scientists have with evolution lies in answering the question, "What caused life in the first place?" It was theorized that life began in an ancient earth environment with chemical-rich oceans and an

---

2008), 189.

   6. Darwin, *On The Origin of Species*, (London J. M. Dent & Sons Ltd, 1971), 167.

   7. Occasionally referred to as the Miller-Urey Experiment after Miller's supervisor, Harold Urey.

atmosphere bombarded with electrical lighting discharges. As Ray Bohlin states, "We have been led to believe that it is not too difficult to conceive of a mechanism whereby organic molecules can be manufactured in a primitive earth and organized into living, replicating cells."[8]

In 1953, Stanley Miller attempted to duplicate a proposed ancient earth scenario in a laboratory using a constant electrical spark (to simulate the lighting) in combination with flasks of chemicals and water, burners, a vacuum pump, and a collection system. The congealed materials produced were tested a week later, and it was determined that there were in fact five nitrogen-containing compounds present (amino acids)—the basic building blocks of life.

Although originally heralded by newspapers around the world as *"Life Has Been Created,"* the reality was that no life had been created. What was synthesized consisted only of a few biochemical compounds and only a single type. Cells consist of millions of different biochemical compounds in different types, such as nucleic acids, amino acids, polysaccharides, and lipids. Forming a couple of amino acid molecules in a beaker is nowhere near biogenesis (the creation of life itself). Producing mindless matter is infinitely different than producing matter with self-replicating capabilities and coded chemistry. In *The Evolution Handbook,* Vance Ferrell reminds us to "Remember that neither nitrogen compounds nor amino acids are, of themselves, living things. Just because they are in living things does not make them living things."[9]

---

8. Ray Bohlin, *Creation, Evolution, & Modern Science: Probing the Headlines that Impact Your Family* (Grand Rapids: Kregel, 2000), 14.
9. Vance Ferrell, *The Evolution Handbook,* 229.

The Stanley Miller experiment is still cited today by many as the answer to how life started, despite the fact that it proved no such thing. More than that, since then it has been commonly recognized in the scientific community that there is no geological evidence to support the idea that the oceans were ever a kind of "organic soup mixture." Additionally, many scientists now recognize that what most likely would have been produced in an electrically charged carbon dioxide, nitrogen and water mix are cyanide and formaldehyde—both of which are lethal to organic life.

Despite Stanley Miller's experiment, and all subsequent testing, the fact remains that scientists don't have the slightest clue how life began. As Bohlin states: "The major difficulty in the field of chemical evolution is how to account for the information code of DNA, without intelligence being a part of the equation."[10] Combining existing chemicals into different forms of matter is no where near the same thing as creating life—a living entity with embedded informational code in its structure and possessing the ability to reproduce. "Living matter possesses an inherent goal or end-centered organization that is nowhere present in the matter that preceded it."[11] No one would ever imagine that a stone, a piece of wood, or even this book would ever become alive, no matter how many millions and millions of years passed. While some still try to cling to the possibility that life can be created by chance combinations of chemicals, the Stanley Miller experiment remains a shattered icon.

> **The problem is that none of the fossil records substantiate Darwin's "Tree of Life" premise, but actually contain evidence against it.**

10. Ray Bohlin, Ph.D., *Creation, Evolution, & Modern Science*, 16.
11. Flew, *There is A God, 124.*

Tree of Life Diagram

In Darwin's book *On the Origin of Species*, there is a diagram that looks like a tree, depicting his theory of how life evolved from simple-celled entities into the limbs, branches, and twigs of the various animal species we see today.[12] The picture, in its portrayal of the slow and gradual ascent of life, has been cited for years in students' textbooks and seems very convincing as a hypothesis for the emergence of the highly variated life forms seen in nature.

The problem is that none of the fossil records substantiate Darwin's "Tree of Life" premise, but actually contain evidence against it. When Darwin was doing his work, almost one hundred and forty years ago, fossils were newly discovered and a cohesive picture of the fossil record had not yet been documented. The picture that is now clear in the fossil record, from the many millions of fossils discovered, is that life did not slowly emerge, but rather that there was an explosion of life in what geologists refer to as the Cambrian Period[13] with over twenty distinct and independent life forms documented as suddenly appearing all at approximately the same time. Although it still stands true in the minds of many, Darwin's "Tree of Life" hypothesis is now widely understood to be in opposition to the fossil record of life.

Ernst Haeckel's Drawings

Ernst Haeckel (1834-1919), a committed advocate of Darwinism, was a teacher at the University of Jena in Germany. Haeckel drew a number of charts that showed

---

12. Darwin, *On the Origin of Species*, 116-17.
13. The author is not endorsing any of the dating claims of the field of geology concerning the Cambrian Period, but instead is merely pointing out the evidence of the fossil record in this layer of rock stratum.

that human embryos were almost identical to other animals'. His premise, and the intention of the charts, was to show that the embryological development demonstrates the transformation of organisms in a type of evolutionary record. He postulated the concept of "vestigial parts"—remnants of organs or body parts that remain in higher level organisms that were "carried over" when they evolved from

> **Haeckel's drawings were very convincing— so convincing, in fact, that despite being complete forgeries, they are still included in science textbooks today as proof of evolution.**

lower level forms of life. In his drawings of embryos, he claimed to observe the presence of gill slits, tails, and other structures that he connected to lower level species like fish, lizards, etc. He called it the *Law of Recapitulation* or the *Biogenetic Law*.

Haeckel's drawings were very convincing—so convincing, in fact, that despite being complete forgeries, they are still included in science textbooks today as proof of evolution. "By the 20th century, reputable scientists recognized that Haeckel's theory was without scientific basis and ridiculous."[14] In 1874, the hoax was exposed when a German embryologist, Wilheim His, Sr., issued a report detailing the fraud. Later, it was learned that Haeckel had actually produced one woodcut and reproduced it three times, labeling the same illustration as "dog," "chicken," and "tortoise." He did essentially the same thing with a picture of an ovum (egg) and labeled them "man," "monkey," and "dog." Ultimately, he was accused of fraud by five professors and convicted by a university court of falsifying evidence.

---

14. Vance Ferrell, *The Evolution Handbook*, 733.

Dr. Michael Richardson, an embryologist at St. George's Medical School in London, says of Haeckel, "This is one of the worst cases of scientific fraud. It's shocking to find that somebody one thought was a great scientist was deliberately misleading."[15]

Amazingly, Haeckel's illustrations about embryonic development and the Biogenetic Law have "become so deeply rooted in biological thought that it cannot be weeded out in spite of its having been demonstrated to be wrong by numerous scholars," writes Walter J. Bock.[16] And thus, Haeckel's drawings, another of the supposed great evidences of evolution, is proven to be fake —another shattered icon.

Missing Link Picture

The theory of evolution is based on the slow and gradual transformation from one species into another. If evolution is true, then there must be extinct intermediate life forms that existed between each distinct species. In Darwin's day, scientists reasonably expected that they would find evidence of these "transitional life forms"—the missing link—in the fossil record. A drawing was made of a series of primates gradually becoming more sophisticated and human-looking, which was meant to depict the missing links as primates slowly morphed into modern man.

> **If life evolved slowly with gradual transitions between species, then the "missing link" shouldn't be missing.**

15. Michael Richardson, *The Times* (London), August 11, 1997, 14.

16. Walter J. Bock, "Evolution by Orderly Law," *Science* 164 (1969): 684–685.

The problem is that now, after many decades of paleontological searching and millions of fossils being found, not a single missing link has ever surfaced. There is a huge gap in the fossil record because it has never produced a single transitional form.

> "The fossil record purportedly contains a record of billions of years of life on earth [with fossils from every epoch]. If it takes 100 million years for an invertebrate to evolve through transitional forms into a fish, the fossil strata should show vast numbers of in-between forms. But it never does!"[17]

The fact is, museums of natural history should be overflowing with fossils that support the theory of evolution— but they don't. If life evolved slowly with gradual transitions between species, then the "missing link" shouldn't be missing. The conclusion must be that the "missing link" is missing because it doesn't exist.

Irreducibly Complex

We now know that all life forms contain biological components and systems that are irreducibly complex. Any system or device is considered irreducibly complex "if it has a number of different components that all work together to accomplish the task of the system, and if you were to remove one of the components, the system would no longer function."[18]

A mousetrap is an example commonly used to explain the concept of an irreducibly complex device. It is a simple mechanical device consisting of five components that must

---

17. Vance Ferrell, *The Evolution Handbook*, 425.
18. Lee Strobel, *The Case for the Creator* (Grand Rapids: Zondervan, 2004), 244.

all work in a coordinated manner in order to catch (kill) a mouse. The five parts consist of a wooden platform, a metal spring, a metal hammer (the component that hits the mouse), a trigger-latch, and a metal catch bar. When the mouse moves the trigger-latch, the tension on the spring causes the catch bar to release the hammer, which in turn hits the mouse, killing it. It is irreducibly complex because you cannot take away any of the parts and still have a functional trap. Every part is essential, and they must all be arranged correctly and working accurately in order for it to operate properly.

Like the mousetrap, there are a number of irreducibly complex biological parts and systems in living organisms. For example, in animals, coagulation—clotting of the blood—is the process that turns blood from a liquid into a gel, in order to stop bleeding and prevent continued loss of blood. The process is an extremely complex cascade of events involving specialized cells (called blood platelets), chemicals, proteins, and enzymes. Remove any one of the essential factors, and the animal can die from a simple wound because their blood can't be stopped from leaking out. Blood clotting is an irreducibly complex system. When all the parts are there, it will work, and if just one is missing, it won't.

There is Nothing Simple About a "Simple Cell"
Hundreds of years ago, single-celled entities were thought of as "simple-celled." Without the aid of modern magnification, the inner workings of the cell were unknown. It was thought that a cell contained nothing more than a balloon-type structure with a cellular wall full of a viscous protoplasmic material.

It is now understood that the cell is a very complex entity. There are very specialized gateways for the entry and exit of materials and products, and complex structures that operate as molecular machines to haul cargo, open and close switches, provide locomotion, and even manufacture products. They operate much like tiny cellular factories. The cell has transport systems, highways, doorways, and engines…even communication systems. These are far from simple, and all of them are irreducibly complex. The myriad of systems must work in perfect harmony, or life ceases to exist.

Evolution Cannot Allow for Irreducible Complexity

Over the course of the last century, people have become increasingly aware of the complexity of biological systems. Organs such as the lungs, liver, kidneys, and eyes are all understood to be irreducibly complex. In addition to organs, tissues, and nerves, we now also know that the same complexity is present on the cellular and molecular levels.

> **Evolution simply does not allow for irreducibly complex biological systems and machines...**

As Michael Behe states:

> "An irreducibly complex system cannot be produced directly… by slight, successive modifications of the precursor system, because any precursor to an irreducibly complex system that is missing a part is by definition nonfunctional. [19]

Evolution simply does not allow for irreducibly complex biological systems and machines because they can't be produced by slow, gradual, and successive modifications of systems that are already existing. The only way it could happen is for a system to suddenly appear, and the odds

---

19. Michael Behe, *Darwin's Black Box; the Biochemical Challenge to Evolution* (Free Press, A Division of Simon & Shuster, Inc., 2006) 39.

are highly against that since natural selection only chooses systems that are already present and functioning.

Intelligent Design

Evolution is a Naturalistic worldview attempt to explain the vast variety of life we see around us. The problem lies in that, as an explanation, evolution seriously fails to answer key matters—such as the origin of life, the lack of transitional forms, and the vast amount of irreducibly complex biological systems. Furthermore, if we are to accept evolution as the *best explanation* for the complex life we see around us, then we must also accept the consequence of that explanation. If life is truly the result of random mutations, then it necessarily follows that there is no intrinsic meaning or purpose to life.

On the other hand, a Supernatural worldview, specifically one that subscribes to the concept of Intelligent Design, provides a very plausible solution to the same questions that evolution fails to answer. Intelligent Design's premise is that the biological structures and systems we observe are not the result of the Laws of Nature or slow and gradual developments. Instead, they are thoughtfully planned and purposefully arranged—hence, Intelligently Designed.

> "The conclusion of intelligent design flows naturally from the data itself—not from sacred books or sectarian beliefs. Inferring that bio-chemical systems were designed by an intelligent agent is a humdrum process that requires no new strategies of logic or science. It comes simply from the hard work that bio-chemistry has done over the past forty years, combined with consideration of the way in which we reach conclusions of design every day."[20]

---

20. Ibid., 193

Evidence of the concept of Intelligent Design surrounds us daily. We live in a world filled with design and we all immediately recognize its presence. Archeologists commonly find buried under layers of soil objects of stone such as arrowheads or spear points, and when they do they immediately recognize them as evidence of the presence of past human activity. Why? Because the stone shows evidence of intelligent design in the way it was chipped and shaped into a useful tool.

In the early 1900's a group of sponge divers discovered an ancient gear-like device about 150 feet under the water. Named after the island where it was found, the Antikythera device is thought to be some type of analog computer used for astronomical purposes.[21] Although it was encrusted with sediment and coral, no one thought, "Look what the coral produced!" The gears and their arrangement pointed toward intelligent design; they pointed to a past civilization of intelligent people.

When it comes to biological systems, we see the very same principles of irreducible complexity and Intelligent Design present. The genetic material present in all living things, whether plant or animal, contains DNA that consists of both matter and information. There is a clear design which holds information in the form of extremely sophisticated codes. This means there must be a source of information behind it. As Behe further states:

"The result of these cumulative efforts to investigate the cell—to investigate life at the molecular level—is a loud, clear, piercing cry of 'design!' The result is so

---

21. https://en.wikipedia.org/wiki/Antikythera_mechanism. Accessed 11/11/15.

unambiguous and so significant that it must be ranked as one of the greatest achievements in the history of science. The discovery rivals those of Newton and Einstein, Lavoisier and Schrödinger, Pasteur, and Darwin."[22]

The Intelligent Design position recognizes that there is an intelligence at work behind the design of the various biological systems we see around us in nature. The similarities in design that Darwin observed between species were not the result of an evolutionary mutation and survival of the fittest, but instead they point to intelligent design crafted by a Designer—a Creator. And the existence of a Creator means that there is a purpose to the creation of life.

---

22. Behe, *Darwin's Black Box*, 232-233.

6

God and Evil

As I mentioned in the beginning of this book, through the years I have talked to many people and discussed with them the reasons why they believe or don't believe in the existence of God. In addition to the apparent conflicts between God and science and God and evolution, a third reason why many people dismiss the idea of God is because of the existence of evil.

When I've presented people with the question, "If you could ask God anything, what would it be?" a fairly common response has been, "Why did You [God] create the world with so much evil?" This is a very legitimate question. After all, if God created everything, then doesn't that mean He created evil, too? For centuries people have tried to reconcile the existence of both God and evil.

What is Evil?

The evil we see in the world can be divided into two types: natural evil and moral evil. Natural evils are physical disasters like tornadoes, hurricanes, tsunamis, earthquakes, etc. These are typically considered "evil" because they are destructive and they hurt and kill people. The other type of evil we commonly encounter is behavioral or moralistic evil. This type of evil describes a person who harms another person, society in general, or even themselves. We all recognize that it is evil for someone to lie, steal, cheat, injure, maim, and kill others. We define those things as evil based upon our morals—our acceptable standards of behavior.

God and Evil Appear to be a Paradox

The presence of evil is truly a conundrum if, as people have traditionally been taught, God is "all-powerful" and "all-knowing." If God is powerful enough to create the physical world, and He also has the ability to know all things, then certainly He should have been able to create a world in which there was no evil. And even if His creation was originally good but then became evil, wouldn't an "all-knowing" and "all-powerful" God have foreseen that outcome and then done something about it? Many people rightly reason that if someone has the ability to do something, but doesn't do it, or if he knows his actions will either directly or indirectly cause harm, but proceeds anyway, then that person is guilty of wrongdoing.

Every adult knows that it is negligent to give a young child a sharp instrument, because there is such a high probability that they will hurt themselves or others with it. It seems reasonable that if this holds true for you and me, then it certainly must be true of God. And from this reasoning, some have responded by saying that if God knew the world was going to be evil, or if He had the ability to stop it and didn't, then they don't want to have anything to do with a God like that.

God Cannot Contradict His Nature

The predicament can be resolved when we properly understand the nature of God, His character, and His relationship with creation. One thing we must understand is that God cannot contradict His nature or act contrary to His character. God has demonstrated that He is loving, morally upright, and good. Some people have proposed that maybe He isn't the "loving God" that people think He is. But if this is true then God is contradicting what He has declared about Himself in Holy Scripture when He says that "He is love."[1] We all know what love is, and it isn't consistent with causing sickness, suffering, or death. We have to consider that the apparent dilemma between God and evil may be a result of our misunderstanding of evil and its source.

As we have done in previous chapters, let's examine this subject from the two different worldview perspectives to see which one, the Natural or Supernatural, has a better explanation for both types of evil we see in the world today.

The Natural Worldview and Evil

In the Natural worldview, since everything that happens is the result of random actions of matter, motion, and chemistry, there is no actual intrinsic good or bad, right or wrong. Everything that happens is merely an event, a chance occurrence without any true meaning or purpose, so there is

---

1. 1 John 4:8, 16

no such thing as the categories of "good" or "evil." Within the Natural worldview it is difficult even to define something as either good or evil, since everything is just a result of the forces of nature.

From the Natural viewpoint, the concepts of good and evil do not really exist; they are merely human constructs, conceptual elements invented by people in order to help describe and manage their world. For a Naturalist, good and evil are considered moral judgments, but any sense we have of something being good or evil is only so because we have socially assigned a moral value to it. Random events and chance interactions are neither good nor evil in and of themselves, they are all simply neutral.

> ...if there is no intrinsic basis upon which we can condemn the acts of people like Hitler or Stalin, similarly, there is no reason to emulate people like Mother Theresa or Nelson Mandela.

When we follow Naturalism to its logical conclusion, we have to accept that there are no such things as intrinsic morals, ethics, or values. There are no absolutes; everything in the realm of values is relative—it is whatever we decide it to be. Something is evil or good only because we, as a society, have decided that it is so, and even then it is not "actually" good or evil. We merely have put a label on behaviors, which have, not surprisingly, changed drastically throughout the centuries according to cultural settings and socially accepted practices.

One of the problems with this line of reasoning is that if there is no intrinsic basis upon which we can condemn the acts of people like Hitler or Stalin, similarly, there is no reason to emulate people like Mother Theresa or Nelson Mandela. On what empirical basis can we truly condemn the murderer or hold the wrongdoer responsible for an act if it is bad merely because society says it is, and it happens only as a result of random interactions? Some Naturalists even go so far as to promote determinism, the belief that all thinking is merely the result of random electro-chemical reactions in our brains, and that the feeling of choice and free will is an illusion.

If, as the Naturalist believes, everything is just matter, motion, and chemistry, then what truly gives anyone the right to determine what is right or wrong? A Naturalist may argue that moral codes have developed for social stability, in order to protect the well-being of the human race. But in a world that is mere matter and random interactions, how can we base anything on the "best interests of society"? Ultimately values, ethics, and morality, as well as crime and punishment become arbitrary concepts, which eventually leads to people not being responsible for their choices and actions.

This is where Naturalism runs headfirst into the brick wall of reality, because our world does not permit people to live free from the consequences of their choices and actions. Even a small child, one who has never been taught the difference between right and wrong or good and evil, knows when a toy is wrongly taken from them. They even perceive when they are in danger, and not because it is a "social construct" they've been taught. Everyone senses that life is better than death; health is preferred over sickness; "good" surpasses "evil." These concepts seem to be far more than mere cultural norms.

When people say something is evil, they are in essence saying that things are not the way they are "supposed to be." It is illogical for a Naturalist to even pose the question on the existence of evil since it makes no sense, *according to their worldview,* that things are *"supposed to be"* any particular way. Similarly, the atheist who questions the existence of God on the basis of evil's existence, by virtue of the question, admits that things are not the way they "should be." The bottom line is that, not only does Naturalism fail to answer the question of evil, it even denies that it exists—except, as some would say, in our minds.

The Supernatural Worldview and Evil

Unlike the Natural worldview, the Supernatural worldview acknowledges the presence of evil and provides a sufficient answer for its existence. Rather than good and evil being mere social constructs, the very fact that we recognize certain actions as "evil" actually argues for the existence of God. The ability of humans to differentiate between good and evil is significant evidence for something in them that guides them to perceive the difference between right and wrong—when life is not as it should be. To the Theist, this is solid evidence for the existence of a moral Creator.

The Supernatural perspective accepts that an underlying standard, a universal truth, exists in the heart of every person and is stirred when we are harmed or wronged. Something deep inside our hearts tells us, "This is not the way things are supposed to be." This inner moral compass guides our navigation and drives us in our desire for justice, for wrongs to be made right, and for evil to be stopped. Therefore, the presence of evil does not pose a problem for the Supernaturalist, and especially not for the Christian Theist.

> Something deeply programmed inside of us tells us that evil is wrong, and we generally seek to rid the world of it.

It is a universal condition that all mankind, no matter if they live in the Amazonian jungles or walk the sophisticated streets of Dubai, can differentiate between good and evil to at least some degree. Something deeply programmed inside of us tells us that evil is wrong, and we generally seek to rid the world of it. The Supernatural perspective acknowledges that people feel something deep within that causes them to applaud the valiant and cheer the hero. On the other hand, we abhor injustice, shun the selfish and avoid the deceitful. Why? Because these are not "social constructs" but part of the fabric of who we are as human beings. This is the Supernaturalist perspective.

Is God Really "All-Powerful"?

The dilemma seems to be that either God is responsible for evil because He made a world in which evil exists, or He should have known evil would occur and done something differently in order to prevent it. This line of reasoning seems simple enough, but we must be open to the possibility that the dilemma exists because of some assumptions we have made concerning the nature of God.

Part of the difficulty we find ourselves in when considering the existence of God and evil is based on our presumption about what it means for God to be "all-powerful." Some have attempted to resolve the conflict by saying that God must not literally be "all-powerful." They reason that God may actually be weak, or at least weaker than people think He is. The rationale is, "If He *could have* gotten rid of evil, He *would have*." This sounds like a plausible argument when considered from a human perspective, but it is also hard to accept that the God who created time, space, all physical matter, and life itself would actually be a *weak* God. Any God who did all that unquestionably should have been able to create the world and all living things without the possibility of evil.

Others promote that God is "sovereign" over all creation, which they believe to mean that he is controlling every aspect of creation, including every person's individual choices and actions. If this is true, then a God who is controlling every aspect of creation, including evil, must be responsible for evil. We can be assured that this is not correct because evil is not consistent with the nature of God who is all good, loving, and kind.

God is sovereign in the same sense that the King of England was that country's sovereign ruler. God is the sole ruler over His creation and like the king, He doesn't control every aspect of His subjects' lives. The citizens have a responsibility to live according to the king's decrees, and if they don't then they are lawbreakers. They alone are responsible for their choices and actions, not the king.

Why Does Evil Exist?

There are a few possibilities to consider concerning the origin of evil. First, there is the possibility that God made the Creation with evil present. But if this is true, then it is an inescapable conclusion that God is directly responsible for evil. This contradicts what God tells us about Himself, which is that He is love, good, light, and that no darkness (evil) exists in Him.[2] In fact, the Bible tells us that God made the world and He considered everything "very good."[3] When God said it was "very good" he was indicating that it was the way He intended it to be: orderly, structured, and under His authority. It could not have been *"very good"* if it was *"very bad,"* too.

Because God tells us that His creation was "very good," we can conclude that God created the world without evil. This must mean that something happened that brought evil into the Creation. The Christian story about the wrong actions of

---

2. Ps. 100:5; Matt. 19:17; Mark 10:18; Luke 18:19; Jas. 1:13; 1 John 1:5.
3. Gen. 1:31

the first humans, also known as the Fall of Man[4], precisely holds that evil is the result of disobedience, both on the part of supernatural beings (angels) and the first man and woman (Adam and Eve).

The reason evil exists is not because God made the cosmos with evil, but because it has become evil. Good and evil are not nebulous terms referring to abstract concepts. "Good," from God's perspective, is a creation that exists according to His intentions and created order. On the other hand, "evil" occurs when things do not proceed according to God's intentions, when there is a state of disorder, disobedience, and even rebellion against God's order and rulership.

The introduction of evil is why we see the entire creation in a state of decay and degradation. This fallen state of creation is referred to when the Bible says that the entire creation "was subjected to frustration" and is waiting to be "liberated from its bondage to decay."[5] The iron that rusts, the wood that rots, and death that eventually attacks and overtakes all living things are precisely consistent with Sir Isaac Newton's Third Law of Thermodynamics, the Law of Entropy, which states that everything is in a state of degradation and unraveling, moving from order to disorder. Even the laws of thermodynamics point to the reason natural and moral evil exist in our world: not because God caused them, but because the world *became* this way.

Love Requires a Choice
What happened to allow evil to enter the world? The

---

4. In Christian theology "The Fall of Man", or "The Fall", are terms used to describe man's initial disobedience to God and the subsequent changes from their state of innocence.

5. Romans 8:20-21

Christian narrative in the Old Testament tells of a time when God created man and woman and gave them rulership and complete control over the earth.

Genesis 1:28
God blessed them and said to them, "Be fruitful and increase in number; **fill the earth and subdue it. Rule over the fish in the sea and the birds in the sky and over every living creature that moves on the ground.**"

God made humankind to have a personal relationship with Him. It was a relationship that was built upon love, and love always requires that a person has the ability to exercise choice. If a person is not capable of making a choice, then they are not free to love or not love, to obey or disobey. Only in freedom, specifically through free will, can a person truly make the choice to love or not love God. God did not want robotic beings that were only programmed to act in a particular way; He desired a genuine and mutual relationship with men and women that was based upon their desire to be with Him, a desire (love) demonstrated through their choices.

> If a person is not capable of making a choice, then they are not free to love or not love, to obey or disobey.

But giving people the ability to choose also meant that there was the risk they could choose to disobey God. God placed a condition upon the first man, Adam, and told him that if he disobeyed, it would bring about death. At one point Adam decided to disobey God in the Garden of Eden, and that act opened the floodgates for evil forces to flow into the world and into the hearts of humanity. Thus, according to the biblical narrative, it was Adam's own actions that caused all of the evil we now see around us.[6]

There is a Cosmic War Between Good and Evil

The Christian position is that there is a cosmic war raging between God and his archrival, the Devil. We are told that God's enemy seeks only to "steal, kill, and destroy," in contrast with God's desire that people would be able to live life to the fullest.[7]

People see evil in the world and blame God for it based on the presumption that God is responsible for that evil. The truth is that there is another spiritual power at work, and it is this enemy of God who is behind all the natural and moralistic evil we see in the world today. This evil force has even been called the "god of this world," a reference to his power and control over the affairs of the earth.[8] Man's disobedience toward God ushered in a time of evil and death. Fortunately, God has a plan that opens the door through which we can escape the power of this evil.

Shouldn't God Have Foreseen the Evil and Done Something to Prevent it?

Some take the position that God is "all knowing," so He should have known that He was creating a world that was going to become evil. Critics of this position reason that if He foreknew that evil was going to occur, and He created the world anyway, then He must be responsible for evil on some level. And further, the fact that evil exists must mean He approves of evil, otherwise He would have done something to prevent it.

---

6. Genesis 1-3
7. John 10:9-10
8. 2 Corinthians 4:4

Although it appears that God knows the future, His "fore-knowledge" is something that theologians and scholars have debated for millennia. The debate rages around the idea of what it means for God to "know" the future. Does He know it in the same way that we know the past and present, or does He merely know it in the capacity to predict it? In either case, we must accept that we are limited in our ability to understand God, and especially His capacity to "know" the future. We are finite beings, having a beginning and an end, but God is eternal, without a beginning or end. How could it even be possible for us as finite beings to be able to understand the infinite?

The entire argument about the extent of God's foreknowledge becomes really irrelevant in discussing its relation to evil because, whether God knows everything or only some things, we know that God's character is love, light, and always good. He also testifies that He made creation to match His character.[9] But why would we assume that the character of creation must then always match the character of the Creator? The fact that the character of creation no longer matches His does not reflect negatively on Him in any way. He did not cause the change in the character of creation. God is not responsible for evil.

> **We can have confidence that God never desired evil, and He isn't the one responsible for it.**

God placed a condition upon the first man, Adam, and told him that if he disobeyed, it would bring about death. Adam had the ability to make a choice to obey or not. He had free will, the ability to make voluntary decisions without coercion or restraint. But giving him the ability to choose meant that there was the risk he could choose to disobey. Thus, according to

---

9. "Let us make man in our image after our likeness" (Gen. 1:26)

the biblical narrative, it was Adam's own actions that caused all of the evil we now see around us.[10]

If this is true, then God's desire for a loving, mutual relationship with mankind was worth the risk that man would choose to disobey Him. Yes, disobedience would introduce evil into the world, but there was also just as much probability that man would love God in return and demonstrate that love through obedience. The greatness of that relationship and that kind of world must have been a risk worth taking. We can have confidence that God never desired evil, and He isn't the one responsible for it. But He has revealed His plan and provision to free mankind from its death-grip upon creation.

---

10. Gen. 3:1-19

Part Two
The Case for Immortality

7

God Loves You and He Wants a Personal Relationship with You

When I headed off to college, I had lots of dreams and aspirations. Although I was just beginning my education, I looked forward to one day graduating with a degree in hand and the doors of employment opportunity open in front of me. I also pictured myself married, with a great career that would allow me to have kids and support a family. On top of that, I tossed in a new car, a nice home, and even a dog.

Everyone in the world lives with dreams and aspirations. Unfortunately, no matter how notable a life we live, if it all ends when we die, then there is no real ultimate point to any of it. The author of the Book of Ecclesiastes stated it correctly:

Ecclesiastes 1:2-4
(2) "Meaningless! Meaningless!" says the Teacher. "Utterly meaningless! Everything is meaningless." (3) What do people gain from all their labors at which they toil under the sun? (4) Generations come and generations go, but the earth remains forever.

As depressing as that may sound, the truth is that life is not meaningless. But the only way for it to have genuine meaning is that God must exist—that there is a Creator who infuses meaning into creation—and our lives must be able to extend beyond our physical death. In other words, immortality must be available, otherwise the moment we die it all comes to a big, permanent "STOP."

And, while it is true that God must exist, there is actually more to it than that. Not only must He be real, He must also be a personal God who desires a relationship with us. Consider that the only alternative to a *personal* God is an *impersonal* One. A personal God is One who wants to have a relationship with humankind, whereas an impersonal God stands apart and is disconnected from, and uncaring toward, His creation. If God were an impersonal Being, then that would almost be no different, and certainly no better, than creation being a result of random, impersonal energy, particles, and motion colliding together.

Man is Lost Because He Fails to Know God
Men and women everywhere roam around filling their

lives with possessions, activities, and endeavors in a futile effort to combat the emptiness in their hearts. This emptiness is a state of meaninglessness, a doomed wandering without purpose. As Christian apologist Francis Schaeffer summarized regarding humankind's state of despair:

> **...man has lost his connection with God and he does not know who God is.**

"The dilemma for modern man is simple: he does not know why man has any meaning. He is lost. Man remains a zero. This is the damnation of our generation, the heart of modern man's problem."[1]

The reason for this state of loss is that man has lost his connection with God and he does not know who God is. Not only does man fail to understand that God exists, but he also fails to know the true character of God. This is why people often attribute to God things that He is not responsible for, such as acts of evil and cruelty. Whenever we falsely accuse someone, or assign to them improper motives for things they have or haven't done, we err because we don't really know the truth about them. The same holds true for God.

The God of Christianity

It is the Judeo-Christian belief that God is a personal God. Religions all over the world promote belief in a god or gods, but most also subscribe to the notion that the god/gods they worship are impersonal and oftentimes cruel, unconcerned, and disconnected from the affairs of humankind, acting with capriciousness and aloofness. These so called "gods" must be appeased and cajoled into providing for the needs of man. They

---

1. Francis A. Schaeffer, *He Is There and He Is Not Silent* (Wheaton: Tyndale, 1972), 10.

are also difficult to understand, and people oftentimes don't know what their gods desire. Unlike these shifting and moody gods, the God of Christianity is a personal God who desires an intimate relationship with every human being and has made it available to know Him, His nature, and His character.

How Can We Know God?

How is it possible for anyone to really know another person? Consider the example of a friend we'll call "George." I know who George is through his words and actions and our encounters together. Others might have told me about George before I personally met him, but they, too, were only relating to me things he said and did.

We know others through their words and deeds which reveal what they like and dislike, their character and the things they value; we also know them through the ethics they demonstrate, whether they have integrity and are reliable or are untrustworthy and untruthful. Jesus told people that they would know others "by their fruits"[2], that is, by their words and actions. In a similar way, we can know God through His words and deeds as well.

The Physical World Reveals God

The cosmos is a finely-tuned entity with the various limits and functions of matter and the different physical forces set to operate within very precise parameters. As mentioned in a previous chapter, all life is totally dependent upon these forces operating harmoniously, within their perfectly set limits. The slightest change would end all life as we know it. When we take the time to closely examine the physical universe around us, we see that God is a God of order, detail, and perfection. He is not a God of chaos and confusion. The intricate details

---

2. Matthew 7:16

of all the provisions He has made point to a Creator who is personal—a God who cares about His creation.

Switching our focus from the cosmos to our planet, we see that Earth functions via systems operating interdependently and with great symmetry. Plants require carbon dioxide for the process of photosynthesis, the by-products of which are carbohydrates and oxygen that animal life depends on. Amazingly, all breathing creatures produce carbon dioxide, the exact gas that plants need in order to survive. This type of interdependence is demonstrated throughout the planet in ecosystems and the natural cycles of wind, water, and geological processes. Once again we see that all of these systems are evidence of a Creator who cares greatly for His creation.

If God truly is the Creator, then the world, as one of His creative acts, must reflect Him and His nature—just like a watch reflects the careful design and intelligence of its maker. When we take the time to ponder the world, we can see the character and nature of God all around us in the intricate details and handiwork of the world. In fact, God even says that humans have no excuse for not knowing or understanding Him because the evidence of His actions is demonstrated throughout the entire physical world.

Romans 1:20
For since the creation of the world **God's invisible qualities—his eternal power and divine nature—** have been **clearly seen**, being understood from what has been made, so that people are without excuse.

There has never been a time in my life when I had to worry about whether or not the sun would rise. The movement of the sun, moon, and all the stars demonstrates God's faithfulness. We know that God is merciful and caring by virtue of the fact that the sun and rain provide for all humankind—not just men and women who love and honor God, but even for those who turn their backs on Him. All of this points to a God who cares greatly for His creation, and most especially for people. His deeds demonstrate that He cares in the exact way we expect that a personal God would.

God Reveals Himself Though Communication

In addition to the physical evidences of the handiwork of God in creation, God has also chosen to reveal Himself to us through words. It is the Christian tradition that the Bible contains the words of God, revealed to humankind so that men and women may know that God exists, and that He rewards those who diligently seek Him.[3]

At one time, anthropologists said that the one thing that distinguished humans from animals was that humans were toolmakers. This is no longer true, though, and they now say the distinction lies in humankind's ability for language. Verbalization—the ability to think and communicate through the use of words—is a domain reserved for mankind alone. Not only do the words used by God convey a message that reveals God's great love and care for humanity, the very fact that God even chooses to communicate with mankind demonstrates that He is personal.

Love is one of the most integral aspects of God's nature.

Through God's words we are even told that the world in which we live is a testament to God's love.

Psalm 19:1-4

(1) The heavens declare the glory of God; the skies

—————————
3. Hebrews 11:6

proclaim the work of his hands.

(2) Day after day they pour forth speech; night after night they reveal knowledge.

(3) They have no speech, they use no words; no sound is heard from them.

(4) Yet their voice goes out into all the earth, their words to the ends of the world.

God's Word and Deeds Indicate that He is a Loving Being

Love is one of the most integral aspects of God's nature. The world we live in, a world that has everything we need to sustain life, indicates that God cares deeply for everyone. This is reinforced by the words He has given us, which also indicate that God loves everyone—every man, woman, and child. Consider the following Bible verses:

1 John 4:7-8

(7) Dear friends, let us love one another, for **love comes from God.** Everyone who loves has been born of God and knows God.

(8) Whoever does not love does not know God, because **God is love.**

God Intimately Knows Each of Us, and Wants Us to Know Him

One of the things that makes a best friend your "best" friend is the fact that they intimately know you—and there is no one who knows and understands you as well as God does.

Psalm 139:13-16

(13) For you created my inmost being; **you knit me together in my mother's womb.**

(14) I praise you because **I am fearfully and wonderfully made;** your works are wonderful, I know

that full well.

(15) **My frame was not hidden from you when I was
made in the secret place**, when I was woven together
in the depths of the earth.

(16) Your eyes saw my unformed body; all the days
ordained for me were written in your book before one
of them came to be.

I think I know my close friends pretty well, but there are
always some things that we don't know about each other.
This is not so concerning God and
us. Jesus even said God knows us so
well that He has numbered the hairs
on our heads.[4]

> God is not
> content that
> mankind would
> merely know
> "about Him," but
> that we would
> be in the closest
> relationship
> possible "with
> Him"

Genuine relationships are never
one-sided. God knows us, but His
desire is that we may know Him
too.[5] God is not content that mankind
would merely know "about Him,"
but that we would be in the closest
relationship possible "with Him"
like the relationship of a parent and a child, because He is a
personal God.

1 John 3:1
See what great love the Father has lavished on us, that
we should be called children of God!

God's Love for Each of Us Knows No Limits
When I was a kid, I had a few really good neighborhood
friends. We were together for years, and none of us ever

---

4. Matthew 10:30
5. 1 John 5:20

imagined that a time would come when we would no longer be friends. But like most kids, as we grew up, went into high school, and eventually moved away from our parents' homes, we all drifted apart. In spite of our best intentions, and no matter how much we all cared for each other, our affection for one another waned as we grew apart. This is not the kind of love God has for us. When we slip and fall it is God's unfailing love demonstrated by His faithfulness that gets us through.

Psalm 36:5
Your love, LORD, reaches to the heavens, your faithfulness to the skies.

Psalm 13:5-6
(5) But I trust in your unfailing love; my heart rejoices in your salvation.
(6) I will sing the LORD's praise, for he has been good to me.

Psalm 94:18
When I said, "My foot is slipping," your **unfailing love**, LORD, supported me.

God Loves Us and He Wants Us to Live with Him Forever

The record of man's beginning in the Book of Genesis tells us that God never desired for death to be a part of creation. Death is the most tragic of all experiences and the most difficult thing for anyone to face. Something deep inside of us tells us that death is bad and should be avoided.

God's original intention when He created man was that he would not die but have everlasting life. God loves us and wants a personal relationship with each of us, but there's a problem. Unfortunately, something cataclysmic happened that interrupted God's plan and separated humankind from God. If we truly desire a life with meaning, we need to understand what happened that was so disastrous that it destroyed the relationship between God and His creation.

8

Man - Separated from God

What could possibly have happened to cause the separation between God and man? After all God tells us that His love for man is so great that it is even "higher than the heavens."[1]

Years ago I realized that trust is like a bridge that connects us to others in relationships. Relationships often start off with a weak and tenuous bridge between people. Then, with each

1. Ps. 108:4

new trust-building action we strengthen the bonds between us and others. Eventually, after years of consistently being trustworthy, we have a solid connection built up. Although it takes a long time to build a solid relational bridge, sadly, it can all be destroyed in mere seconds when trust is violated. Given the distance mankind now feels from God, something monumental must have happened to break the original trust between God and man.

Hosea was an Old Testament prophet who gave us a clue about the breakdown. In the Book of Hosea he recorded God saying, "Like Adam, they [speaking of Israel] have broken the *covenant*; they were unfaithful to me there" (Hos. 6:7 NIV 84). God was making a direct comparison between Adam's breaking his agreement with God, and Israel doing the same. Everyone understands the concept of a promise: it is an assurance that we will do, or not do, something. But a "covenant," as used by Hosea, is not a word that we commonly use nowadays. A covenant is actually much more than a promise.

People frequently break their promises, such as a promise to meet a friend at a certain time or the promises we make to do something for someone else. A covenant however is much stronger than a promise, in that it is a *legally binding agreement* involving *mutual benefits* and *consequences* for all the participants. What Hosea was saying was that there was a binding agreement between God and Adam. Just like Israel was breaking their agreement with God, so too Adam broke the agreement he had with God.

What was the Agreement Between God and Adam?

In the book of Genesis, we find many details of the agreement God had with Adam. In essence, God told Adam that he was to "rule" over all the earth and its creatures, and he was to be "fruitful and increase in number," meaning to fill the earth with his offspring. He was also to subdue the remainder of the earth, the area outside the Garden in which God had placed him.[2]

There was a Condition

Along with the benefits of rulership, God told Adam that there was one condition: he was forbidden from eating of the Tree of the Knowledge of Good and Evil, and the consequence for breaking this condition would be death. In essence, Adam's obedience to the one condition God placed on him would demonstrate that he made the freewill choice to submit himself to God's ultimate rulership over the Creation.

Adam was made morally upright and, like a small child who has never experienced harm and evil, he had a pure nature and innocence. He had the freedom to choose to obey or disobey, and through the choice he made God could know whether Adam truly loved Him or not. God entrusted His creation to Adam—and remember, the economy of their relationship, like all relationships, depended upon the currency of trust.

Genesis 2:9
The LORD God made all kinds of trees grow out of the ground—trees
that were pleasing to the eye and good for food. **In the middle of the garden** were the **tree of life** and the **tree of the knowledge of good and evil.**

Genesis 2:16-17
(16) And the LORD God commanded the man, "You are free to eat from any tree in the garden;

---

2. Genesis 1:26, 28; 2:7-8

(17) but you must not eat from the tree of the knowledge of good and evil, for **when you eat** from it **you will certainly die."**

The Consequences of Disobedience

Through acceptance of the rulership and dominion over the Earth, Adam accepted the terms of the covenant with God. Breaking that covenant brought very severe consequences—so severe that they actually changed the physical nature of the Creation, resulting in an existence for man that required hard toil and sweat for food, and, worst of all, introduced death into the world.

> **Adam and Eve's treasonous act against God was so great that the entire nature of the Earth was affected.**

Genesis 3:17-19
(17) To Adam he said, "Because you listened to your wife and ate fruit from the tree about which I commanded you, 'You must not eat from it,' **"Cursed is the ground** because of you; through **painful toil you will eat food** from it all the days of your life.
(18) It will produce **thorns and thistles** for you, and you will eat the plants of the field.
(19) By the **sweat of your brow** you will eat your food until **you return to the ground**, since from it you were taken; for dust you are and to **dust you will return."**

Prior to Adam and Eve's disobedience to God, the earth was a place of safety and beauty. This all changed after their disobedience, when they were no longer in a state of moral purity. Their disobedience (sin) introduced evil into the world in ways that they never imagined.

Thorns, Thistles, and Death

The record of Genesis tells us that the world changed in some very dramatic ways after Adam sinned. Some plants began to produce thorns and thistles

All the evil in the world rests solely upon the shoulders of man and the Devil.

and, where once Adam and Eve had been able to "eat freely from the trees" in the Garden, now they had to work the land with "painful toil" and "sweat of the brow" to produce their food.

Another result of the sin of Adam and Eve was that Eve would have to endure painful childbirth. We can assume that "painful childbirth" is not something God originally intended for women, but it is certainly the reality of childbirth for women now.

Genesis 3:16

To the woman he said, "I will make your **pains in childbearing very severe**; with **painful labor you will give birth to children**. Your desire will be for your husband, and he will rule over you."

Adam and Eve's treasonous act against God was so great that the entire nature of the Earth was affected. We are told the Earth entered into a state of slavery to decay, metaphorically speaking as if it were groaning in labor pains as it waits for the day when it can be "liberated from its bondage."

Romans 8:20-22

(20) For **the creation was subjected to frustration**, not by its own choice, but by the will of the one who subjected it, in hope

(21) that the creation itself will be **liberated from its bondage to decay** and brought into the freedom and glory of the children of God.

(22) We know that **the whole creation has been**

groaning as in the pains of childbirth right up to the present time.

Even the rulership of the Earth, once mankind's sole responsibility, was transferred to another. This is why God says that the whole world is now under the control of the Evil One.[3]

Frequently people want to blame God for all the evil in the world, but this is much like the crowd blaming the baseball umpire when the batter strikes out. The fault lies solely upon the player. Like God, the umpire is merely enforcing the rules of the game. All the evil in the world rests solely upon the shoulders of man and the Devil.

One of the Greatest Disasters was Death

As horrific as it would be to have to leave Paradise and to work hard for food, to have to deal with the pain of thorns and thistles and childbirth, this was nothing compared to the ultimate consequence—death. God was clear with Adam when He told him that disobedience would result in death. The rule was simple: if you disobey (sin), you will die.

Romans 6:23
The **wages of sin is death...**

When I work at my job, at the end of the pay period I am compensated according to the wages I agreed to work for. In the same way, God and Adam agreed that the wages of his disobedience would be death. This is a spiritual law that God established and it has never changed. When anyone sins, what he or she deserves as a consequence is death. This is why since Adam first disobeyed death has reigned over mankind.

---

3. 1 John 5:19 (NIV 2011)

Romans 5:14
Nevertheless, **death reigned from the time of Adam**
to the time of Moses, **even over those who did not
sin by breaking a command, as did Adam**, who is
a pattern of the one to come.

Romans 5:17
For if, **by the trespass of the one man, death reigned
through that one man...**

Death is an inescapable reality for all people. Through
the sin of Adam, death entered into the world and has had
rulership ever since over every man, woman, and child. We
have all sinned so, like Adam, we too all deserve the wages
of sin, which is death.

Romans 3:23
For all have sinned and fall short of the glory of God,

Man was Separated from God

No matter how much Adam wanted a relationship with
God, the consequences of his violation of God's trust caused
such irreparable damage that it was no longer possible.
Along with Adam's newfound knowledge of good and evil
came a corruption of his nature and character. Prior to his
disobedience, Adam enjoyed an open and honest relationship
with God. Immediately after he disobeyed, we see that he hid
from God, cowering from Him because he was filled with fear
and shame. Both Adam and Eve lost their innocence and took
on the new nature of the Evil One with his craftiness.

Being Good Isn't Good Enough

The average person who believes in Heaven will tell you
that being a "good person" is what's required to get you there.
The problem with being a "good person" is that no one can be

quite good enough. Why not? Because *good* is not determined by you or me, but by God, and His standard of what is good far exceeds our understanding.

God set the standard, and ever since Adam's "Fall" none of us can meet it. Ask yourself, "Have I ever told a lie, taken something that didn't belong to me, cheated anyone, gossiped, or thought lustfully about another?" These are some pretty minor things, and certainly some of us are guilty of even more egregious behaviors than these. The answer is, "Of course I've done some of these things; we all have." Remember that the spiritual law established in the beginning was, "Sin results in death." This means that since you've sinned, even as minor as you want to make it, you deserve death for it. It is a non-negotiable law, which is why our "good" just isn't *good enough.*

> **Bridging the gap between mankind and God is something we cannot do on our own; it requires a special repair...**

Not only have we all personally sinned, Adam's sin was so disastrous that it caused irreparable damage to the entire human race, both physically and spiritually. The physical effects resulted in suffering, disease, and death, and the spiritual effect was humanity's propensity to sin. Unfortunately, everyone has inherited the guilt of Adam's sin, which is also why, no matter how well we live our lives, none of us is capable of restoring the relationship that was lost with God.

God Has a Plan

What is the answer to the problem of death? No matter how much anyone wants to restore the relationship with God, no one is able to because our very nature has been changed. The relationship between man and God was broken, and mankind lacks the ability to rebuild it. Like a bridge that has collapsed over a canyon that is too wide and deep to cross, the repair requires specialized engineering knowledge and mechanical abilities. Bridging the gap between mankind and God is something we cannot do on our own; it requires a special repair—something that is far beyond our ability. This is why we require God's help.

The good news is that God, as the Master Architect and Builder, had a plan, a design and the means to rebuild the bridge between Himself and mankind. In the next chapter we will look at the specifics of God's plan and how we can now walk across the bridge—if we so choose.

9

God Has a Plan

Like someone lost in a cave without a torch, groping about in the pitch darkness, all mankind is disconnected from God and is futilely searching for meaning and purpose in life. Adam and Eve's disobedience to God was so devastating that the aftershock from the collapse of the relational bridge between them is still felt by mankind today. Since then, neither the physical world nor mankind has been the same. The Bible is a story of God's plan for restoring the bridge and how He has gone about its construction.

Sin Creates a Debt

When we do something harmful, we have a responsibility to correct the situation, to make it right with the party that has been harmed. Our sin creates a debt with God that needs to be paid. This is not only true for behavior like lying or stealing, it holds true for all wrongful actions. Whenever we cause relational damage with others, there are things we need to do to attempt to repair the damage. Oftentimes we even say that someone "owes" to make it right with the other person. We sense when a relational imbalance has been created and, like a debt that is owed to another, we must make payment to make it right again.

> ...God told him [Adam] beforehand that if he sinned, the damage would be so great that the price was death...

In the case of Adam's sin, God told him beforehand that if he sinned, the damage would be so great that the price was death—a debt so high that only a qualifying life could pay it. Worse, like a rock tossed into the waters of a calm lake, Adam's sin rippled out, touching every future generation.

God Had to Intervene

The problem Adam's disobedience caused was so great that it required God to intervene. God had a plan for a bridge to span the chasm between Himself and man and He knew it would require a lot of time and effort to build. God also stepped in and allowed mankind to offer the lives of animals for the debt of sin, but that was only paying the interest on the mortgage. Animal sacrifice was a temporary solution; something more would be required to fully satisfy this debt.

God Reveals His Plan to Man

God's plan was first revealed when He informed Adam and Eve that one of their descendants was eventually going to come who would destroy the Serpent (the Devil), who had deceived them and brought sin into the world.

Genesis 3:15
And I will put enmity between you and the woman, and between your offspring and hers; **he will crush your head**, and **you will strike his heel**."

Although the Serpent would "strike his heel," the one who would pay the debt of humankind would deliver a mortal wound to him when he "crushed his head." Striking someone's heel will hurt a lot, but a crushed head is a fatal blow. From that day forward, mankind knew there was the hope of a special Redeemer coming in the future who would fix the problems that the first man, Adam, had caused.

The Bible is a Record of God's Plan and His Moves to Bring About His Plan

Everything in the Bible, aside from the first few chapters, is a record of God's plan and the moves He has made throughout history to bring it to pass. In the pages of the Bible, God reveals His plan to send a man, a very special man, who alone would have the proper qualifications to pay the debt Adam and Eve had created. Even though God told Adam and Eve that this man was coming someday, no one would have any idea who he was, unless of course God described for them who they should be looking for.

How Will We Know Who the Redeemer is?

A number of years ago, I needed to find a construction jobsite on a remote stretch of the highway that leads to Lake Tahoe in northern California. It is a rural stretch of roadway that winds through the mountains with the river on one side and the mountain slopes covered in evergreen trees on the other—not an easy place to find a site. In order to find jobsites there we always had to rely on detailed descriptions of landmarks and use mile markers. In a similar way, God gave mankind various signs to be on the lookout for. God said He was sending a man to repair the damage between God and mankind, but like a traveler without a roadmap, how would people know who he was when he came?

Over thousands of years, God provided various descriptions of this Redeemer. These signs involved his family background, where he would come from, where he would live, and things that he would do and say. These descriptions were given to prophets in the Old Testament; collectively there are over 300 of them. The Jews knew this man as the Messiah, meaning the "deliverer" or "savior"—he was going to deliver mankind from the predicament Adam had placed us in.

Prophetic Signposts

Throughout history God has provided some very clear signposts concerning the lineage of the Redeemer. He would be a man, just as Adam was, and also like Adam, God would be his Father. The following are some of the specific details of his family bloodline.

1. He Must Be a Human, from the Race of Adam

Concerning His Lineage

While Adam and Eve were still in the Garden, God gave them the promise that He was going to send someone who would straighten out the mess they had created (Genesis 3:15, as quoted previously). Essentially the message was spoken to the Deceiver: that the woman was going to have a child and, although the Serpent would harm him, he would destroy the Serpent.

In this message, God revealed that the one who was

coming would be an "offspring" of the woman, meaning that he would be a human descendant of Eve. The Serpent would harm him (striking his heel) but he would eventually kill the Serpent (crushing his head).

The first Adam messed up God's creation, and it was only through a "second Adam" that man could be redeemed and creation be put back in order. In the Letter to the Romans, the Apostle Paul gave the insight that the first Adam was a "pattern" of the Messiah, which is why at times Jesus is referred to as the "second Adam."

Romans 5:14
Nevertheless, death reigned from the time of Adam to the time of Moses, even over those who did not sin by breaking a command, as did **Adam, who is a pattern of the one to come**.

The authors of the book *One God & One Lord* provide the following insight:

"There are many people in the Old Testament who could be called "types of Christ." But this is the only place in the New Testament that directly points back to a particular person who set *the* pattern for who the Messiah would be like. Adam was a "...pattern of the one to come...")"[1]

The first signpost is clear: the Messiah would be a man just like the first Adam, and he would be an offspring of the woman. Though the Serpent would harm him, the Messiah would eventually deliver a death blow to him.

---

1. Graeser, Lynn, and Schoehnheit, *One God & One Lord*, 4th ed. (Indianapolis: Spirit & Truth Fellowship, 2010), 17.

2. His Lineage Would Be Traced Through a Specific Human Family

As time went on, God disclosed that the Savior would come through a specific family line. This narrowed the possibilities considerably from the whole human race down to a select bloodline. Around 400 years after the flood of Noah, God selected a man named Abraham, and because Abraham completely trusted Him, God promised him that he would be the father of a great nation and that "all peoples would be blessed through him." This was a prophetic indication that the Redeemer would come from Abraham's bloodline because of his faithfulness to God.

Genesis 12:2-3
(2) "I will make you into a great nation, and I will bless you; I will make your name great, and you will be a blessing.
(3) I will bless those who bless you, and whoever curses you I will curse; and **all peoples on earth will be blessed through you."**

This promise was made to Abraham so that he could instruct his children and household on the ways of God. The intent was that his offspring would be faithful to God, and that through them God could bring about the Redeemer.

Genesis 18:17-19
(17) Then the LORD said, "Shall I hide from Abraham what I am about to do?
(18) Abraham will surely become a great and powerful nation, and **all nations on earth will be blessed through him.**
(19) For I have chosen him, so that he will direct his children and his household after him to keep the way

of the LORD by doing what is right and just, so that the LORD will bring about for Abraham what he has promised him."

In tracing Abraham's descendants, we see that God renewed this promise to Abraham's son Isaac, and again to his son Jacob. After Jacob, the promise was made to his son Judah, who was the patriarch of one of the twelve tribes of Israel. We can trace this through various passages in the Book of Genesis.[2]

3. The Messiah Would Be Called "The Son of David"

Over 900 years after Abraham, God again made an unconditional covenant with David in which He promised that the Messiah would come from David's descendants and, like David, he would be a king—but his kingdom would endure forever. Once again God narrowed down the possibilities of the Messiah's lineage. (2 Sam. 7; 1 Chron. 17:11-14; 2 Chron. 6:16)

4. The Son of God

One of the most essential requirements for a man to be the Redeemer of mankind was that he would have to have God as his Father. The phrase "Son of God" is a very specific term reserved for beings that are directly created by God. Consider the following explanation by John Schoenheit:

The [phrase] 'son of God' in the Hebrew is *bene Elohim*, which is simply the sons of God, *bene*: son of (you might remember the movie Ben Hur. The man in the movie was Judah ben Hur, Judah the son of

---

2. Genesis 17; Genesis 26

Hur) and *bene Elohim* is a son of God. If you check
the Old Testament in the Bible, when someone was a
'son of God,' a *bene Elohim*, they were in some way
created or formed by God. Adam, the first man ever,
who had no mother and father, is called in Luke 3:38,
in the genealogy, a 'son of God.' Notice that none of
the other men in the genealogies of the Old Testament
were called 'sons of God.'[3]

In order for Jesus to be a Son of God, He would have
had to create in Jesus' mother the genetic material normally
contributed by the male. When the angel Gabriel appeared
to Mary announcing God's intention to bring the Redeemer
through her, she asked, "How will this be since I am a virgin?"[4]
The angel described the possibility in the following way:

Luke 1:35
The angel answered, "The Holy Spirit will come on you,
and the power of the Most High will overshadow you.
So the holy one to be born will be called the Son of God.

This was a fulfillment of the prophecy of David:

Psalm 2:7
I will surely tell of the decree of the LORD: He said to
me, `Thou art My Son, today I have begotten Thee.'"

5. A Perfect Sheep from the Flock

It was the first man, Adam, who violated the covenant he

---

3. John Schoenheit, "The Sons of God of Genesis Six." Accessed
August 24, 2015; http://www.truthortradition.com/articles/the-sons-of-
god-of-genesis-six
4. Luke 1:34

had with God, and therefore it would require another man to restore that breach. Since the penalty for the disobedience was death, it would require the death of a perfect sacrifice to pay this price. God provided an example of this sacrifice through the Jewish Feast of Passover. The Jews were instructed that a sheep had to be taken from the flock, just as the coming Messiah would be from the flock of humanity. Like the Passover lamb for the feast, the Messiah would have to be perfect and without blemish, meaning without spiritual, physical, or moral defect. (Exod. 12:3-13)

Concerning the Redeemer's Birth and Upbringing

In addition to Jesus' bloodline from Judah, to David, and finally through Mary, there were also specific prophetic signposts about his mother, his place of birth and upbringing, and the conditions surrounding his childhood.

6. Born to a Young Woman

As a result of improper translations of the Hebrew text, many Christians believe that the Prophet Isaiah foretold that the Redeemer would be born to a virgin. What Isaiah had actually stated was that a "young woman will conceive and give birth to a son and will call him Immanuel,"[5] although the testimony of the Scripture is that Jesus' mother was both a young woman and a virgin.

7. Born in Bethlehem

The Prophet Micah provided the prophetic signpost that the Redeemer would be born in Bethlehem.

---

5. Isaiah 7:14 (RSV)

Micah 5:2
"But you, **Bethlehem** Ephrathah, though you are small among the clans of Judah, **out of you will come for me one who will be ruler over Israel, whose origins are from of old, from ancient times.**"

8. The Slaughter of Children

One of the most horrific details surrounding the infant years of Jesus is the story of how King Herod, jealous and concerned about protecting his throne from a usurper, sought out the location of the coming Redeemer King and attempted to kill him by slaughtering all the children two years old and younger in the vicinity of Bethlehem. This genocide was foretold by the Prophet Jeremiah:

Jeremiah 31:15
This is what the LORD says: "A voice is heard in Ramah, mourning and great weeping, Rachel weeping for her children and refusing to be comforted, because they are no more."

9. Called from Egypt

Joseph, Mary's betrothed, was warned by an angel in a dream to flee to Egypt because of Herod's plans to kill all the children in Bethlehem. When Joseph, Mary, and Jesus returned to Judea after the death of King Herod, this fulfilled the prophecy that the Redeemer would be called out of Egypt (Hos. 11:1).[6]

10. He Would Come from Galilee

---

6. Although most understood that the words of the Prophet Hosea were directed at the nation of Israel, his prophecy also included the Redeemer.

Returning from Egypt, Jesus' parents decided not to return to Bethlehem in Judea, but instead to go north and settle in Nazareth in the region of Galilee. In doing so, they fulfilled the prophecy of Isaiah which foretold that the Messiah would come from the area of Galilee in northern Israel. (Isa. 9:1-2)

Concerning His Actions

11. He would Speak in Parables

One of the ways that God has kept things from the plain sight of humankind is by using riddles and obscure sayings. The Serpent deceived Eve as part of his attack against God and God's desire for humankind, so God has had to employ this technique to keep things obscured from His enemy, too. David foretold that the Messiah would speak in parables (Ps. 78:2).

12. He Would Be a Prophet Like Moses

God worked with Moses to perform some astounding signs, miracles, and wonders as he sought to have Pharaoh release the Israelites from their Egyptian captivity. He also delivered the Law to him and was with him throughout the Israelites' 40-year wandering in the wilderness. As the time of Moses' death approached, speaking of the Messiah, Moses foretold that God would raise up another prophet like himself (Deut. 18:15).

13. He Would Have Zeal for the Temple and Would Act with Authority

The Redeemer's love and obedience toward God resulted in his great offense at seeing the Temple turned into a marketplace with money changers and vendors taking advantage of those who came to worship and offer the required animal sacrifices. It is recorded that Jesus drove them out with a scourge as he uttered the same words Jeremiah foretold: "Has this house, which bears my Name, become a den of robbers to you?" (Jer. 7:11)

14. He Would Ride into Jerusalem on a Donkey

The prophet Zechariah foretold that the Messiah would enter Jerusalem as a king riding on "a donkey, on a colt, the foal of a donkey" (Zech. 9:9 NIV 2011).

15. He Would Make the Blind to See, the Deaf to Hear, and the Lame to Walk

It was understood that when the Redeemer came, there would be great healing. The goal was that humankind's relationship with God would be restored and that the damage caused by sin, such as disease and death, would be reversed. When Jesus came, he made the blind to see, the deaf to hear, and the lame to leap for joy, just as Isaiah had prophesied (Isa. 35:5-6).

Concerning the Messiah's Suffering and Death

We can see from the many details God provided ahead of time that He didn't want anyone to be mistaken about the identity of the man He was going to send. What is even more amazing are the many things foretold about the details surrounding the Messiah's death. Listed below are some of those details and the scripture references of the prophecies:

16. **Hated without cause** (Psalm 35:19)
17. **Rejected by men, mocked** (Psalm 69:9; Psalm 22:7, 8)
18. **Betrayed by a close friend** (Psalm 55:12-13; Zechariah 11:12)
19. **Sold for 30 pieces of silver** (Zechariah 11:12)
20. **Falsely accused** (Psalm 35:11)

21. **Silent in front of accusers** (Isaiah 53:7)
22. **Crucified with criminals** (Isaiah 53:12)
23. **Hands pierced and crucified** (Zechariah 12:10)
24. **None of his bones broken** (Psalm 34:20)
25. **Side pierced** (Zechariah 12:10)
26. **Clothing would be gambled over** (Psalm 22:17)
27. **Given gall to drink** (Psalm 69:21)
29. **Darkness would be over the land** (Amos 8:9)
30. **Buried in a rich man's tomb** (Isaiah 53:9)

What Are the Odds?

One of the most interesting aspects of the Bible is that it contains a lot of predictive prophecy—the foretelling of events before they happened. In fact, a significant portion of the Old Testament is predictive, possibly as much as twenty-five to thirty percent. It is very noteworthy that, with the exception of those things concerning Jesus' second coming in the future and the end times, he fulfilled every single one of the 300-plus prophecies about the Messiah. What are the odds that any one person could have done that?

Life is filled with probabilities and statistical odds. For instance, what are the odds that you will be struck by lightning today? Scientists tell us the odds are 1 in 250 million that it will happen to any given person on any given day. They have also been able to calculate the odds of you being struck by lightning in your entire lifetime, which is 1 in 9,100. That's a tremendous increase in the probability that it will happen, which makes sense when you add up all the individual days in a year and multiply that by the average person's lifespan. They have also calculated the odds of you being struck by a meteor at 1.8 in 10^{14}—that is 10 followed by fourteen zeros, which is really a rather large number.

So what are the odds that one man would fulfill all of the

various prophetic signposts that God gave ahead of time? As each prophecy was made, the principle of compound probability dictated that the likelihood of one person fulfilling all of them decreased. In the book *Science Speaks,* Peter W. Stoner and Robert Newman calculated the odds using the following eight of the over 300 prophecies given about the Messiah. Below is the summary of the calculations Stoner and Newman made to determine exactly what the odds are that one man would fulfill these eight prophecies.

1. Born in Bethlehem (1 in 2.8 x 100,000)
2. John the Baptist coming before (1 in 1,000)
3. Entering Jerusalem on a donkey (1 in 100)
4. Betrayed by a friend (1 in 1,000)
5. Sold for 30 pieces of silver (1 in 100,000)
6. Pieces of silver used to buy the Potters field (1 in 100,000)
7. Silent during trial (1 in 1,000)
8. Crucified (1 in 10,000)

Stoner and Newman make the following conclusion:

"If these estimates are considered fair, one man in how many men, the world over, will fulfill all eight prophecies? This question can be answered by applying our principles of probability. In other words, by multiplying all of our estimates together, or 1 in 2.8 x 10^5 x 10^3 x 10^2 x 10^3 x 10^5 x 10^3 x 10^4. This gives us 1 in 2.8 x 10^{28}, where 28 means that we have 28 ciphers following the 2.8. Let us simplify and reduce the number by calling it 1 in 10^{28}. Written out this number is:

1 in 10,000,000,000,000,000,000,000,000,000."[7]

7. Peter W. Stoner and Robert Newman, *Science Speaks,* chapter

What does this really mean? How can we relate to something with odds like this? This would be like painting one silver dollar black and then placing it in an area the size of Texas, covered two feet deep with other silver dollars. The odds are the same as you reaching blindfolded into that mass of silver dollars and pulling out the one black one. Any one person who fulfilled just the eight prophecies listed above had to be the One that God said would come to restore the bridge between Himself and humankind.

> **...the odds that one person would fulfill 48 of the prophecies is 1 in 10^{157}.**

And in case those odds and probabilities haven't gotten your attention yet, the odds that one person would fulfill 48 of the prophecies is 1 in 10^{157}. This is the same as finding one particular atom in a ball the size of the universe, and then repeat that 100,000 times—in other words, it can't be done.

In physics, scientists consider any occurrence taking place with the odds beyond 10^{50} as something that must be true, because the odds are so great in favor of it happening that for it not to happen is "manifestly absurd."[8] Now bearing in mind that Jesus didn't fulfill just eight prophecies (1 in 10^{28}), or even just forty-eight (1 in 10^{157}), but that he actually fulfilled over 300 prophetic signs. The odds are so high in his favor that he absolutely has to be the One, and for him not to be is *manifestly absurd!*

> **The odds are so high in his favor that he absolutely has to be the One, and for him not to be is manifestly absurd!**

3, "The Christ of Prophecy." Accessed 8/27/2015; http://sciencespeaks. dstoner.net/Christ_of_Prophecy.html#c9

8. "Absurd" has a mathematical definition in physics: any probability less than 1 in 10^{50} is, by definition, absurd. 12-5-2015. http://www.khouse.org/articles/1998/163/#notes

Jesus is God's Plan for Mankind

God said He was sending someone, and the signposts are clear for us to see that Jesus is the One who God planned to save humankind. God said that Jesus would die as a sacrifice for the disobedience of all humankind, but God also said He would raise him from the dead.[9] God was able to do this because Jesus, with God as his Father, was not under the curse of Adam, and since he never disobeyed God, he didn't deserve death.

> **Hebrews 9:26-28**
> (26) …he has appeared once for all at the culmination of the ages to **do away with sin by the sacrifice of himself**.
> (27) Just as people are destined to die once, and after that to face judgment,
> (28) so **Christ was sacrificed once to take away the sins of many;** and he will appear a second time, not to bear sin, but to bring salvation to those who are waiting for him.

> **Ephesians 5:2**
> Christ loved us and gave himself up for us as a fragrant **offering and sacrifice to God.**

> **1 John 2:2**
> He is the **atoning sacrifice for our sins**, and not only for ours but also **for the sins of the whole world.**

God Wants to Give Everyone the Gift of Everlasting Life

God has made His intentions clear: He wants everyone to have the gift of immortality.

---

9. Ps. 16:10; 30:3; 49:15

1 Timothy 2:4
Who [God] wants all people to be saved and to come
to a knowledge of the truth.

John 3:16
For God so loved the world that he gave his one and
only Son, that whoever believes in him **shall not
perish but have eternal life.**

The only questions that remain are, "Do I want to live
beyond my physical death?" and if so, "What must I do to
receive everlasting life?"

10

The Gift of Immortality

    Over twenty years ago, as I was driving to work one day, I came across a horrific traffic accident on the highway. At first I didn't think much about the traffic slowing down because, like the typical California commuter, I was accustomed to frequent accidents on the Golden State's crowded highways. Thankfully, most of these accidents consist of a crumpled fender, maybe a minor neck whiplash or other injury, and they only involve a few vehicles; but often traffic backs up for miles when people slow down to gawk and try to take in every shocking detail as they pass the scene.

Looking ahead this time, I saw the sea of bumpers turn red as everyone's brake lights flashed on, signaling that something up ahead was wrong. Traffic slowed to a crawl, and as I slowly inched closer I began to see twisted metal and car parts strewn across the roadway. Just as I came to the site of the wreck, I noticed a blanket on the roadway, clearly out of place. I didn't realize that I was holding my breath as I grasped that the blanket covered the body of a woman, her bare foot poking out from underneath as if sun bathing in the bright morning light. My mind flooded with a cascade of thoughts and emotions as I drove on past her lonely high-heeled shoe where it lay cast aside, no longer of any use to its owner.

> **For the most part, we ignore death, its ugliness and its ever-present reality.**

I remember thinking in that moment, "This poor woman is lying like a piece of trash abandoned in the middle of a highway. She must have a family, maybe even a husband and children, and they have no idea that she's dead." I imagined her readying herself for work only a short time earlier, maybe making her children breakfast and kissing them goodbye as she headed off to work, unaware that she would soon be involved in a fatal accident. How could she have had any inkling of what fate awaited her on the highway that day? Just like her, how can any of us have the faintest notion of what awaits us in a week, a day, or even in the next few minutes? The reality is, we can't!

Death—and Our Refusal to Really Accept it

For the most part, we ignore death, its ugliness and its ever-present reality. Within five minutes of passing that horrible scene of death, I had pushed it out of my mind as I rolled on down the highway. I turned my thoughts to my workday, the phone calls I needed to make and the people I planned on seeing. Isn't pushing death into the back recesses of our minds something that we all do, much like the quickly-disappearing scenery in the rearview mirror.

Let's face it: nowadays our culture insulates us from the grim realities of death. No longer do we personally kill and butcher animals for their meat; instead we go to supermarkets where we buy nice, sanitary, prepackaged cuts of chicken, beef, and pork in their handy little cellophane-wrapped, Styrofoam trays. No longer do we have to see the animal die, enduring the smell of death and the grimy and often disgusting task of cleaning and gutting it. Our need and craving for animal protein requires that they die, but God forbid we should really think of how it happens and what it takes to obtain meat from them. We have disconnected ourselves from the daily presence of death, and in so doing we have done ourselves a great disservice.

Even when our loved ones die, most do so in a hospital setting behind closed doors, where they are secretly whisked down the corridors camouflaged on a specially-designed gurney so that no one has to see the body. Modern science has even made it possible for the mortician to skillfully apply his macabre craft with pink fluids and makeup so that the dead don't even appear dead, but instead look as if they are merely sleeping. But no matter how hard we try to hide, deny, and avoid it, death is real, and it waits around the corner for us all.

Are You Prepared for Death?

Corresponding to the joy of every birth is the sadness of one more death. No one escapes it. So the one question everyone needs to ask themselves is, "Am I prepared for death?"

Death has only two possible outcomes. If the Materialist or Naturalist worldview is correct, then when we die, we cease to exist completely, in which case there is nothing we need to do to prepare ourselves, because there is no meaning or purpose to life. On the other hand, if the Supernaturalist view is correct, specifically the Christian worldview, then there is life beyond the grave, in which case preparation for death is of primary importance.

God's Plan

Thankfully, although God promised death would come due to Adam's disobedience, He also promised to send a way to help humankind to conquer death— a way to have immortality.

> ### Romans 6:23
> For the wages of sin is death, but **the gift of God is eternal life** in Christ Jesus our Lord.

God was very clear with Adam when He told him that if he disobeyed, the consequence would be death. He never wanted this fate for humankind. Informing someone of the consequences of their actions is not the same as wanting those consequences to come to pass. If a parent instructs a child that touching a hot object will burn them, and then the child touches it anyway and gets burned, it was not because the parent wanted or caused it to happen. Adam derailed God's plan for a personal relationship with humankind, and death has had rulership over man ever since.

> ### Romans 5:14
> Nevertheless, **death reigned from the time of Adam to the time of Moses, even over those who did not sin by breaking a command, as did Adam,** who is a pattern of the one to come.

There is Only One Way to God

There is an old adage that says, "All roads lead to Rome." While that may have been true of Ancient Rome, it's not true of God. Religious pluralism is the view that all religions are basically the same, and all equally valid. It has become very popular to think this way about spirituality and God, and while there may even be some merit to the idea that many religions are basically the same, there are several important differences between them, too.

I once heard a man use an example showing two pills held in the palm of his hand. Both were the exact same size, shape, and color, and most agreed that they looked identical. The problem was that one pill was an aspirin, but the other was cyanide. Holding the pills out for all to see, he asked, "Should we be more concerned about the similarities or the differences between them?" Clearly the differences are what matter, since one pill will cure your headache and the other will kill you.

> **What is it that Jesus is going to save people from? He saves us from death...**

Like the two pills, isn't it true that we should have more concern for the differences between religions than their similarities? Certainly they can't all be true when they make conflicting claims. God never said that He was going to send "many redeemers" to solve the problem of death. Instead, He said He was sending a single Redeemer. All religions can't lead us back to God when He said there was only going to be one way. Jesus cut right to the chase when he said:

John 14:6
"I am the way and the truth and the life. No one comes to the Father **except through me."**

In the first century, the followers of Jesus who had lived daily with him spread the same message. After Jesus' departure, Peter stood before a very large crowd and proclaimed that Jesus is the only way to be saved.

Acts 4:11-12
(11) Jesus is 'the stone you builders rejected, which has become the cornerstone.'
(12) **Salvation is found in no one else, for there is no other name under heaven given to mankind by which we must be saved.**

What is it that Jesus is going to save people from? He saves us from death by giving those who put their trust in and follow him everlasting life. Jesus made it very clear: whoever believes in him will receive the gift of everlasting life, and whoever rejects him will not.

John 3:36
Whoever believes in the Son has eternal life, but **whoever rejects the Son will not see life**, for God's wrath remains on them.

A number of years later, Jesus' followers were preaching the very same message. The Apostle Paul, one of the principle leaders of the first-century Church, wrote the following to his young protégé Timothy:

1 Timothy 2:5-6
(5) For there is one God and **one mediator** between God and mankind, the man Christ Jesus,
(6) who gave himself as a ransom for all people. This has now been witnessed to at the proper time.

As popular as religious pluralism may be today, it is

diametrically opposed to what Jesus taught. It isn't politically correct nowadays to say that what someone else believes is wrong. It is true that people have the right to believe anything they want, but that doesn't mean that what they believe is actually true. Religious pluralism may make people feel good about being able to choose what they think is right, but according to Jesus, it is still wrong.

There is Only One Bridge

I grew up in a small town north of San Francisco, California. Occasionally I would ride along with my dad when he went across the Golden Gate Bridge into San Francisco. The bridge spans a gap of about three miles, and prior to its construction there was no way to cross except by ferry or by driving hundreds of miles around the bay, a trip that would take virtually an entire day. I was always impressed as we crossed the wide gap in the land with the churning waters of the San Francisco Bay below us. The immense bridge with its huge towers and massive suspension cables is an engineering marvel that took many years and thousands of workers to build.

> **God desires that every man, woman, and child would accept His invitation to cross from death to life.**

The Golden Gate Bridge reminds me of the bridge God needed to build between humankind and Himself. The gap was so wide and treacherous, seemingly insurmountable; then God's Son came, and by laying down his perfect sinless life as a sacrifice for all of humanity, the bridge was built.

John 5:24

"Very truly I tell you, **whoever hears my word and believes** him who sent me **has eternal life and will not be judged but has crossed over from death to life.**

The only sure way to be prepared for death is by knowing God, the Author and Creator of life, and His Son, Jesus Christ, the perfect sacrifice for all humankind.

John 17:3
Now this is eternal life: that they [the world] know you, the only true God, and Jesus Christ, whom you have sent.

God's Free Gift to Mankind — Grace!
God's bridge cost an unimaginable price to build, but unlike the Golden Gate, this bridge requires no toll fee to cross. There is nothing anyone can do to earn passage. God extends the gift of free passage to all who want to cross.

Ephesians 2:8-9
(8) For it is by **grace you have been saved**, through faith— and this is not from yourselves, it is the gift of God—
(9) not by works, so that no one can boast.

How Do We Receive This Gift?
The hard part of building the bridge has already been done. God desires that every man, woman, and child would accept His invitation to cross from death to life. All we need to do is to accept His free gift. The way to do this is stated simply in the following passage:

Romans 10:9-10
(9) If you **declare with your mouth, "Jesus is Lord,"** and **believe in your heart** that **God raised him from the dead**, you will be saved.
(10) For it is with your heart that you believe and are justified, and it is with your mouth that you profess your faith and are saved.

First, we declare Jesus as our Lord, which means that we submit to Jesus, giving him the rulership over our lives. Previously, we have done as we have wanted—we were the masters of our own lives. Now, we confess Jesus as our Master and decide to follow his ways and teachings. The only other condition is that we truly believe in our hearts that God has raised Jesus from the dead.

Once we've done that, we cross from death to life. We are completely prepared for physical death, in the sense that now our future will not cease when we die. Instead, we now have the free gift of everlasting life.

Romans 10:11-13
(11) As Scripture says, "**Anyone who believes in him** will never be put to shame."
(12) For there is no difference between Jew and Gentile—the same Lord is Lord of all and richly blesses all who call on him,
(13) for, **"Everyone who calls on the name of the Lord will be saved."**

Sons of God
At the moment of our salvation, when we believe and receive the free gift of everlasting life, we become God's children.

1 John 3:1
See what great love the Father has lavished on us, **that we should be called children of God!** And that is what we are! The reason the world does not know us is that it did not know him.

God adopts us as His own children through His spirit that He gives to those who have put their trust in Him and in His Son Jesus Christ, the Redeemer whom He sent to save us.

Romans 8:14-16

(14) For those who are led by the Spirit of God are the children of God.

(15) The Spirit you received does not make you slaves, so that you live in fear again; rather, the Spirit you received brought about your adoption to sonship. And by him we cry, "Abba, Father."

(16) The Spirit himself testifies with our spirit that we are God's children.

Make the Choice for Life

We believe there is evidence all around us that supports the belief that God exists. His existence is not in conflict with science or the existence of evil. The evidence also leads us to believe that He is a personal God, wanting a personal relationship with you, His creation. As soon as death entered His creation, God set in motion His plan to redeem humankind. It is available now for everyone to have immortality by believing in the work of His Son, Jesus Christ.

When I think of life and death, I am reminded of a particularly beautiful day I once experienced. It was one of those days when the temperature was just right, not too hot and not too cold. The sun was shining, the trees were gorgeous in their bloom and the lawns were majestic, a sea of green swells rolling to the horizon. I even pictured the songbirds singing hymns on this special occasion. People made their coffee, kissed loved ones goodbye, and headed to work. But for me and several people I knew, it was also a day when we gathered to say our final goodbyes and to honor the life of a good friend who had passed away. Despite all the beauty and life around us that day, we were confronted with the stark reminder that all life ends in death.

> **What we can control... is whether or not death will be the end of us.**

But is death the final chapter in our life's story?

No one has any control over their birth, and we certainly have little control over the day and hour of our death. What we can control, however, is whether or not death will be the end of us. God has made it available to cross the bridge from everlasting death to everlasting life by accepting His Son, Jesus Christ. Accepting the sacrifice Jesus made for you shows that you know your life has genuine purpose and meaning, and that you are prepared for the day you die because you have been guaranteed that the show is not over yet—everlasting life is yours:

John 3:16
"For God so loved the world that he gave his one and only Son, that **whoever believes in him shall not perish but have eternal life**"

Consider Jesus as the answer, and choose to receive the life that is waiting for you.

"We truly have nothing to lose…and infinite to gain!"

What is Spirit & Truth Fellowship International®?

Spirit & Truth Fellowship International (STFonline.org) is a ministry that is teaching, training, and networking likeminded Christians around the world who desire to make known the Good News of the Lord Jesus Christ. As a legal entity, we are a non-profit, tax-exempt United States (Indiana) corporation.

Our Vision Statement is: "Building an Enduring Work of Truth." Our vision is demonstrated through various strategies that are anchored in our four core values of truth, integrity, courage, and liberty.

Our Mission Statement is: "To provide sound, biblically-based teaching and training to equip and empower Christians, and to facilitate a network of likeminded individuals, fellowships, and churches."

Spirit & Truth Fellowship International is accomplishing its overall mission by way of live speakers, audio and video teachings, books, seminars, websites, camps and conferences. Our biblically based teachings and networking point people toward an intimate relationship with the Lord Jesus Christ, and are designed to promote personal spiritual growth.

Spirit & Truth Fellowship International has its Home Office in Indiana and assists the networking of fellowships around the world (STFonline.org/churches). Our partners and supporters are Christians who freely affiliate themselves with us because they are in general agreement with our doctrine and practice, and want to be a part of spreading these truths around the world.

Our name is partially derived from Jesus' statement in John 4:23 and 24 that God is seeking people to worship Him "…in spirit and in truth." The basis for all our efforts is the Bible, which we believe to be the Word of God, perfect in its original writing. So-called errors, contradictions, or discrepancies are the result of man's subsequent interference in the translation or transmission of the text, or his failure to understand what is written.

Spirit & Truth Fellowship International draws from all relevant sources that shed light on the integrity of Scripture, such as geography, customs, language, history, and principles governing Bible interpretation. We seek the truth without respect to tradition, "orthodoxy," or popular trends and teachings. Jesus declared himself as the truth, and stated that knowing the truth would set one free. Our vision of "Building an Enduring Work of Truth" is in obedience to Jesus' command to "…go and make disciples of all nations..." (Matt. 28:19).

Any individual willing to examine his beliefs in the light of God's Word can profit from our teachings. They are non-denominational, and are intended to strengthen one's faith in God, Jesus Christ, and the Bible, no matter what his denominational preference may be. Designed primarily for individual home study, the teachings are the result of intensive research and rational methods, making them easy to follow, verify, and practically apply.

If you like what we are doing and you would like to help us continue to spread the Gospel all over the globe, please consider sowing into our ministry at: STFonline.org/donate

CPSIA information can be obtained at www.ICGtesting.com
Printed in the USA
LVOW10s0345160816

500507LV00007B/16/P